Praying the Psalms

Praying the Psalms

Walter Brueggemann

A PACE Book
Saint Mary's Press
Christian Brothers Publications
Winona, Minnesota

Photo credits: John Arms, page 38; Steve Murray, page 14; Ron Sievert, page 66; Vernon Sigl, pages 26, 50; Erik Simonsen, cover

Printed in the United States of America

Printing: 10 9 8 7 6 5 4
Year: 1993 92 91 90 89 88 87

Library of Congress card catalog number 81-86045
ISBN 0-88489-143-7

For
Lila Bonner Miller

Contents

Preface

Psalm study among the scholars has been on something of a plateau for some time. The dominant positions of Hermann Gunkel on form-critical matters and Sigmund Mowinckel on cultic context are still in place. There has been little scholarly movement beyond their brilliant proposals that would link scholarly work to the life of the Psalms in the Church.

But more recently there have been important contributions in developing the connections between scholarship and Church. Among the most important of these are Bernhard Anderson, *Out of the Depths* (Philadelphia: Westminster Press, 1974) and Claus Westermann, *The Psalms: Structure, Content and Message* (Minneapolis: Augsburg Press, 1980). More popularly, see also Thomas H. Troeger, *Rage! Reflect, Rejoice!* (Philadelphia: Westminster Press, 1977). And there is more to come out of the fertile suggestions of Rainer Albertz and Erhard Gerstenberger, whose works await translation.

The present book does not attempt to go over the consensus of scholarship again. Rather than repeat so much material covered in many handbooks, here the work of Gunkel and Mowinckel is assumed. Nor do we need to review the extensive secondary material derived from that consensus. This book attempts to address only two specific issues which hopefully will aid in reading the Psalms both more knowingly and more passionately.

The first issue concerns the function of *language* in the use of the Psalms. It is clear that conventional exegesis will not make contact with the compelling power of the poetry of the Psalms. And that failure about language in large part is the cause of the gap between the scholarly consensus and the vast array of "devotional materials." I have not spent time here on the foundations of linguistic function to which I appeal. I have tried to show how the Psalms might be liberated for more poignant and faithful use if we will grant the language of the Psalms the imaginative and free play for which it must have been intended. I claim no expertise on linguistic theory. But it will be evident that I have found the work of Paul Ricoeur most helpful and stimulating. A more comprehensive statement of my presuppositions and my utilization of Ricoeur is given in "Psalms and the Life of Faith: A Suggested Typology of Function," *Journal for the Study of the Old Testament* 17 (1980): 3-32.

The second issue considered is the Christian use of poetry which is *obviously Jewish*. It is clear that the next efforts in Christian theology must concern interaction with Jewish faith. Undoubtedly Jewish faith is problematic for Christians. Concerning the Psalms, Christians (in practice if not in theory) deal with the Jewish "awkwardness" either by cunning selectivity or by knowing spiritualization. Either way, such use misses the point. It is of course hazardous for a Christian to make a statement about the Jewishness in these texts. I have taken a risk about that and perhaps have not done it rightly. But I hope my statement, if it is enough on target, may contribute to the urgent interface of Christian worship and Jewish faith. And even if not right, I hope it is clear that I have acted in good faith.

On both the questions of the *liberation of language* and *Jewish awkwardness*, very much is at stake for the Church. I hope to contribute to the vitality of the Church's faith by pointing to the subversive and powerful resources available in the Psalms. It is an unreformed Church which uses the Psalms for a domesticated spirituality. It is not an accident that the Reformers of the sixteenth century attended to the Psalms in intensive ways. On both questions taken up, I have reference to "the one from whom no secret can be hid." On the one hand, I have urged that language here is not only for candor but for the articulation of that which is known both by God and by human persons only when articulated. That is, everything depends on the articulation, for such speech evokes something quite new for both parties in the conversation. That no secret can be hidden depends on such risky articulation.

On the other hand, I have argued that such candor is no empty, neutral form but has a distinctively Jewish shape—the shape of active, protesting suffering; the shape of defiant, resilient hope. The *stuff* of Jewish suffering and Jewish hope is a unique partner to the *form* of strident, subversive, intense forms of language. That is, this bold *form of speech* peculiarly matches the *Jewish practice* of suffering and hope. It is the interplay of the *stuff of Jewish faith* and the *form of Psalmic speech* which might matter to the spirituality of the Church.

I should say a word about how this little book came to be. It is as spotty and selective as it is because it was originally a series of separately printed papers. They were written at the behest of Mary Perkins Ryan, who has had them published in *Professional Approaches for Christian Educators* (PACE) by Saint Mary's Press. The pieces were not intended to be comprehensive or complete; they are only suggestions along the way in reading and praying the Psalms. I have intended that these suggestions should be not only exegetical but hermeneutical as well. Mary Perkins Ryan has been a strong and supportive editor, and I am delighted to express my thanks to her. If these papers do not quite amount to a well-argued book, their original intent and purpose must be kept in mind.

We have determined to include in this publication a copy of the Psalms so that they are immediately available for ready reference as the book is read and studied. We felt the convenience and additional value for the reader definitely warranted the additional cost factor. We have decided to use the Revised Standard Version simply because it probably has the widest usage among readers of the book.

The dedication is to Lila Bonner Miller, M.D. She combines in her life and psychotherapeutic practice all the abrasive candor of liberated faith and all the certitude of unflinching trust that belongs to this tradition. She was formed in the Psalms in the practice of the Associate Reformed Presbyterian Church. Not only has she remained in that nurture—she has practiced the Psalms in bold ways, with both her spirit and her mind (1 Cor. 14:15). That is a great gift to many persons, including this son-in-law.

Walter Brueggemann
Eden Seminary
Rosh Hashanah (1980 C.E.)

Praying the Psalms

Chapter 1:

Letting Experience
Touch the Psalter

We pray together regularly "for all sorts and conditions of men" (and women), as the Book of Common Prayer puts it. We know all about those sorts and conditions, for we are among and like all those others. When we pray for all those others, we pray for ourselves along with them. We are able to pray for the others precisely because we share a "common lot." They are like us and we are like them in decisive ways. Thus one way of knowing about "all sorts and conditions of men" and women is to be attentive to what is happening in our own lives.

A second way in which we know about those others is to be attentive to what is written—in the daily newspaper as well as in great literature. The daily newspaper is a summary and chronicle of what goes on among us, the healings and betrayals, the reality of power sought and gained, of broken-ness and gifts and victories. All of that belongs to these "sorts and conditions" for whom we pray.

In addition to our own experience and the testimonies of print, the Psalms of the Old Testament offer a third presentation of how it is with all sorts and conditions of men and women. The Psalms, with a few exceptions, are not the voice of God addressing us. They are rather the voice of our own common humanity—gathered over a long period of time, but a voice that continues to have amazing authenticity and contemporaneity. It speaks about life the way it really is, for in those deeply human dimensions the same issues and possibilities persist. And so when we turn to the Psalms it means we enter into the middle of that voice of humanity and decide to take our stand with that voice. We are prepared to speak among them and with them and for them, to express our solidarity in this anguished, joyous human pilgrimage. We add a voice to the common elation, shared grief, and communal rage that besets us all.

In order to pray the Psalms, our work (liturgy is indeed work) is to let our voices and minds and hearts run back and forth in regular and speedy interplay between the stylized and sometimes too familiar words of *Scripture* and our *experience* which we sense with poignancy. And when we do, we shall find that the words of Scripture bring power, shape, and authority to what we know about ourselves. Conversely, our experience will bring to the words of Scripture a vitality and immediacy that must always be reasserted within the Psalter.

Beyond Our Time of Equilibrium

Before turning to the Psalms, let us consider what are those "sorts and conditions" which are true of all of us and which come to speech in the Psalms. I suggest, in a simple schematic fashion, that our life of faith consists in moving with God in terms of (a) being securely *oriented*, (b) being painfully *disoriented*, and (c) being surprisingly *reoriented*. This general way of speaking can apply to our *self*-acceptance, our relations to significant *others*, our participation in *public issues*. It can permit us to speak of "passages," the life-cycle, stages of growth, and identity crises. It can permit us to be honest about what is happening to us. Most of all, it may provide us a way to think about the Psalms in relation to our common human experience, for each of God's children is in transit along the flow of orientation, disorientation, and reorientation.

The first situation in this scheme, that of being securely

oriented, is a situation of equilibrium. While we all yearn for it, it is not very interesting and it does not produce great prayer or powerful song. It consists in being well-settled, knowing that life makes sense and God is well placed in heaven, presiding but not bothering. This is the mood of much of the middle-class Church. In terms of the Bible, this attitude of equilibrium and safe orientation is best reflected in the teaching of the old Proverbs which affirm that life is equitable, symmetrical, and well-proportioned. This mood of humanness is minimal in the Psalms but may be reflected in Ps. 37, which is mostly a collection of sayings that could as well be placed in Proverbs. And the same is more eloquently reflected in such a marvelous statement as Ps. 145, which trusts everything to God. Such Psalms reflect confident well-being. In order to pray them, we must locate either in our lives or in the lives of others situations of such confident, buoyant, "successful" living.

But that is a minor theme in the Psalms and not very provocative. The Psalms mostly do not emerge out of such situations of equilibrium. Rather, people are driven to such poignant prayer and song as are found in the Psalter precisely by *experiences of dislocation and relocation*. It is experiences of being overwhelmed, nearly destroyed, and surprisingly given life which empower us to pray and sing.

In the Rawness of Life

Recently there has been considerable discussion of those events which drive us to the edge of humanness and make us peculiarly open to the Holy One. This investigation, pertinent to our theme, is undertaken because many persons conclude that the "religious dimension" of their life is void. And so there is an asking about those elements in our life that relate to the "hunger for transcendence." In a variety of ways, it is suggested that the events at the edge of our humanness, i.e., the ones that threaten and disrupt our convenient equilibrium, are the events which may fill us with passion and evoke in us eloquence. Thus the Psalms mostly reflect such events of passion and eloquence when we are pressed by experience to address the Holy One.

We have noted the convergence of (a) our experience, (b) the account of the newspaper, and (c) the Psalms as being articulations of our deep human experience. But we should distinguish the Psalms in one important point as being different. Unlike our own experience and that of the newspaper, it is the Psalms which present "all sorts and conditions of men" and women *addressed to the Holy God.* Thus the events at the edge of humanness which are so crucial for us and which are reflected in the Psalms tend to (a) evoke *eloquence,* (b) fill us with *passion,* and (c) turn us to the *Holy One.* As we enter into the prayer and song of common humanity in the Psalms, it is helpful to be attentive precisely to the simple eloquence, the overriding passion, and the bold ways in which this voice turns to the Holy One.

And what situations drive us to the edge of our humanness? They are situations of extremity for which conventional equilibrium offers no adequate base. Peter Berger[1] refers to these extremities as experiences which are filled with "rumors of angels," i.e., hints of some surplus of meaning. He suggests they include experiences of order, play, hope, damnation, and humor.

Langdon Gilkey[2] speaks of experiences of "contingency" when we become aware of how precarious our life is and aware also of the inexplicable givenness of it. For him, these dimensions include an experience of givenness, threat, limitedness, value, freedom, and condemnation. Paul Ricoeur[3] refers to "limit-experiences." Following Karl Jaspers, he includes death, suffering, guilt, and hatred, but they may also include " 'peak experiences,' especially experiences of creation and joy which are no less extreme than are experiences of catastrophe." Reference to Berger, Gilkey, and Ricoeur tells us something important about prayer, especially in the Psalms. Reflect for a moment on the coined phrases of "rumor of angels," "the whirlwind," "contingency," "limit-experiences." In different ways, all these writers—a sociologist, a theologian, and a philosopher interested in psychology—all of them are pointing to the deep discontinuities in our lives where most of us live, on which we use most of our energies, and about which we are regularly preoccupied.

Thus we follow them in suggesting that it is the experiences of life which lie beyond our conventional copings which make us eloquent and passionate and which drive us to speak to the Holy One. And it is experiences beyond conventional orientations which come to vivid expression in the Psalms. That is what we mean by "all sorts and conditions of men" and women—that we have to do here with the powerful, dangerous, and joyful rawness of human reality. And in the Psalms, we find the voice that dares to speak of these matters with eloquence and passion to the Holy One. Psalms offer speech when life has gone beyond our frail efforts to control.[4]

Note that the Psalms thus propose to speak about human experience in an honest, freeing way. This is in contrast to much human speech and conduct which is in fact a cover-up. In most arenas where people live, we are expected and required to speak the language of safe orientation and equilibrium, either to find it so or to pretend we find it so. For the normal, conventional functioning of public life, the raw edges of disorientation and reorientation must be denied or suppressed for purposes of public equilibrium. As a result, our speech is dulled and mundane. Our passion has been stilled and is without imagination. And mostly the Holy One is not addressed, not because we dare not, but because God is far away and hardly seems important. This means that the agenda and intention of the Psalms is considerably at odds with the normal speech of most people, the normal speech of a stable, functioning, self-deceptive culture in which everything must be kept running young and smooth.

Against that, the speech of the Psalms is abrasive, revolutionary, and dangerous. It announces that life is not like that, that our common experience is not one of well-being and equilibrium, but a churning, disruptive experience of dislocation and relocation. Perhaps in our conventional, routinized prayer life (e.g., the daily practice of the office) that is one of the reasons the Psalter does not yield its power—because out of habit or fatigue or numbness, we try to use the Psalms in our equilibrium. And when we do that, we miss the point of the Psalms. Moreover, our own experience may be left untapped and inarticulate and therefore not liberated. Such surface use of the Psalms coincides with the denial of the discontinuities in our own experience. Ernest Becker has written of *The Denial of·Death.*[5] But such denial happens not just at the crisis points. It happens daily in the reduction of language to numb conventions.

Thus I suggest that most of the Psalms can only be appropriately prayed by people who are living at the edge of their lives, sensitive to the raw hurts, the primitive passions, and the naive elations that are at the bottom of our life. For most of us, liturgical or devotional entry into the Psalms requires a real change of pace. It asks us to depart from the closely managed world of public survival, to move into the open, frightening, healing world of speech with the Holy One.

Lament as Speeches of Disorientation

So let us consider in turn the experiences of *disorientation* and *reorientation* which characterize human life and which are the driving power of the Psalms. If we move from the premise of equilibrium, we may speak of *chaos* (disorder) and *new order.* And these are elemental dimensions, both to our experience and to the Psalms. The Psalms, by and large, emerge from and reflect precisely such situations of chaos and new order. And any attempt to take these speech-events of chaos and new order and make them instruments of conventional equilibrium is a travesty. To make the Psalms serve "business as usual" misunderstands the Psalms, even though habitual use of them has tended to do just that.

So first, the reality of chaos, disorder, disorientation. Each of us knows about that in our own life. It may be a visible issue like a marriage failure, the loss of job, a financial reverse, the diagnosis of the doctor. Or it may be nothing more than a cross word, a disappointing letter, a sharp criticism, a minor illness. Or it may be disturbance of a public kind, anxiety over the loss of energy, revulsion at the sickening spectacle of war, the sense that the world is falling apart before our very eyes, the unspeakable horror of a possible nuclear war. It may be the discovery of loneliness, the sense of being rejected and unloved. All or any of these is the awareness that life is not whole, that it is not the romantic well-being which we were taught in Sunday School and which is so shamefully and shrewdly reflected in television ads. Indeed the world is a dangerous, frightening place, and I am upset for myself. And when I can move beyond my own fear and grief, I do not need to look far to find the hurt and terror others have, whether these others are my own friends or people I see and hear about on TV.

The Psalter knows that life is dislocated. There need be no cover-up. The Psalter is a collection over a long period of time of the eloquent, passionate songs and prayers of people who are at the desperate edge of their lives. The stylized form of such speech is the lament Psalm, of which there are many examples in the Psalter. The best known is Ps. 22. The neatest, simplest example is Ps. 13. The angriest, most hopeless is Ps. 88, which ends in unreserved, unrelieved gloom.

Thus I propose a direct link between the *experience of dislocation* in which we all share and the *lament Psalm* of Israel. There are those who know about disorientation but have no speech which can adequately say it. But there are also those (and this is our primary concern here) who face the lament Psalm but do not bring to it the raw disorientation which is all about us and which is the intended agenda of the Psalm. It is the work of the one who prays a Psalm to be actively engaged in holding this linkage in a conscious, concrete way. For when we do, we discover that this Psalm is affected by our experience, and even more surprising, we find that our experience has been dealt with by the Psalm.

We must not make these Psalms too "religious" or pious. Most of the lament Psalms are the voice of those who "are mad as hell and are not going to take it any more." They are not religious in the sense that they are courteous or polite or deferential. They are religious only in the sense that they are willing to speak this chaos to the very face of the Holy One. Thus the lament Psalm, for all its preoccupation with the hard issue at hand, invariably calls God by name and expects a response. At this crucial point, the Psalm parts company with our newspaper evidence and most of our experience, for it is disorientation *addressed to God.* And in that address, something happens to the *disorientation.*

The Surprising Songs of Newness

The other movement of human life is the surprising move from disorientation to a new orientation which is quite unlike the old status quo. This is not an automatic movement which can be presumed upon or predicted. Nor is it a return to the old form, a return to normalcy as though nothing had happened. It is rather "all things new." And when it happens, it is always a surprise, always a gift of graciousness, and always an experience which evokes gratitude. It may be thought that in our daily experience the events of reorientation are not as frequent as are the times of dislocation. Perhaps that is so. Perhaps we have not learned to discern the ways the wondrous gift is given. We dare to say that in our existence there is the richness of life along with the reality of death. There is the power of resurrection as well as the inescapability of crucifixion. The conquest of chaos and the gift of fresh life-giving order must also be brought to speech. Such experiences include all those gifts of friendship and caring, all those gestures of reconciliation and forgiveness, all those risky signs of hope in public life—the initiative of Sadat in Jerusalem, the bold women in Ireland who march for peace, the great festivals of reconciliation in the Church—all experiences which may touch us deeply and announce that God has not left the world to chaos (cf. Isa. 45:18-19).

These events we may not notice unless we practice the language of praise and thanks. And for this, the Psalter offers us the celebrative language of hymns and songs of thanksgiving,[6] which sometimes assert the abiding rule of God as in Ps. 103, but at other times announce the surprising intrusion of God who just now makes things good (Ps. 114). That is what is meant in those Psalms which announce that "God is King" (Pss. 96:10, 97:1, 98:6, 99:1). They celebrate some experience which has brought the world to a new joyous orientation which is experienced by the speaker. Thus I suggest that there is a linkage to be maintained between the *experiences of reorientation* and Israel's *Psalms of thanksgiving and hymns.* There are those who have a sense of the new gift of life and lamentably have no way to speak about it. But there are also those (and this is our primary concern here) who have regular access to the Psalms of high celebration but have been so numbed to their own experience that the words of the Psalm have no counterpart in their own life experience.

The collection of the Psalter is not for those whose life is one of uninterrupted continuity and equilibrium. Such people should stay safely in the Book of Proverbs, which reflects on the continuities of life. But few of us live that kind of life. Most of us who think our lives are that way have been numbed, desensitized, and suppressed so that we are cut off from what is in fact going on in our lives.

The Psalms are an assurance to us that when we pray and worship, we are not expected to censure or deny the deepness of our own human pilgrimage. Rather, we are expected to submit it openly and trustingly so that it can be brought to eloquent and passionate speech addressed to the Holy One. If we are genuinely attentive to these linkages of speech and experience, we will discover that we pray a prayer along with our brothers and sisters in very different circumstances. Others may give a different nuance to their speech, but they also have the realities of disorientation and reorientation in their lives. And they thus join in this resilient voice addressed to the Holy One. The Psalms are not used in a vacuum, but in a history where we are dying and rising, and in a history where God is at work, ending our lives and making gracious new beginnings for us. The Psalms move with our experience. They may also take us beyond our own guarded experience, into the more poignant pilgrimages of sisters and brothers.

Notes

1. Peter L. Berger, *A Rumor of Angels* (Anchor: Doubleday and Co., 1970).

2. Langdon Gilkey, *Naming the Whirlwind* (Indianapolis: Bobbs-Merrill Co., 1969).

3. Paul Ricoeur, "Biblical Hermeneutics," *Semeia* 4 (1975): 108-135.

4. Anticipating Ricoeur in important ways, Karl Barth wrote: "It is no accident that of all the books of the Old Testament the Psalter has always been found the most relevant. This is not in spite of the fact, but just because of it, that in so many passages it echoes the people of the covenant trembling for its preservation in final extremity before its all-powerful enemies. The Christian community always has good reason to see itself in this people, and to take on its own lips the words of its helpless sighing, the cries which it utters from the depths of its need. It turns to the Psalter, not in spite of the fact, but just because of it, that as the community of Jesus Christ it knows that it is established on the rock (as powerfully attested by the Psalms themselves), but on the rock which, although it is sure and impregnable in itself, is attacked on all sides, and seems to be of very doubtful security in the eyes of all men and therefore in its own." Karl Barth, *Church Dogmatics IV, 2* (Edinburgh: T & T Clark, 1958), p. 671.

5. Ernest Becker, *The Denial of Death* (New York: The Free Press, 1973).

6. On the cruciality of thanksgiving for the faith and worship of Israel, see the fine discussion by Harvey Guthrie, *Theology as Thanksgiving* (New York: Seabury Press, 1981).

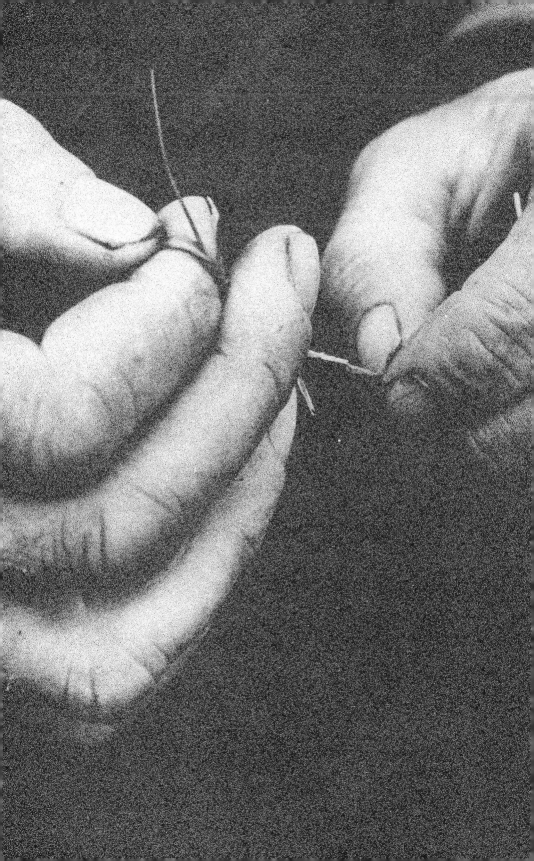

Chapter 2:

The Liberation of Language

Praying the Psalms depends upon two things: (1) *what we find* when we come to the Psalms that is already there and (2) *what we bring* to the Psalms out of our own lives. In our first chapter, we have urged that when we come to the Psalms *we shall find* their eloquence and passion and boldness in addressing the Holy One. Further, we have urged that what *we bring* to the Psalter in order to pray is a candid openness to the extremities in our own lives and in the lives of our fellows, extremities which recognize the depths of despair and death, which acknowledge the sheer gift of life.

The work of prayer is to bring these two realities together—the boldness of the Psalms and the extremity of our experience—to let them interact, play with each other, tease each other, and illuminate each other. The work of prayer consists in the imaginative use of language to give the extremities their full due and to force new awareness and new configurations of reality by the boldness of our speech. All this is to submit to the Holy One in order that we may be addressed by a Word that outdistances all our speech.

A Language Adequate to Experience

Let us begin with a presupposition about language that is necessary to entering into the Psalms. In our culture, we imbibe a positivistic understanding of language. That is, we believe that the function of language is only to report and describe what already exists. The usefulness of such language is obvious. It lets us be precise and unambiguous. It even lets us control. But it is one-dimensional language that must necessarily be without passion and without eloquence and indeed without boldness. It is useful language, but it is not the language we have in the Psalms. Indeed it is not the language in which we can faithfully pray. Such language is useful for managing things. But it makes no impact on how things really are, for things would be the same even if there were no such speech.

By contrast, in the Psalms the use of language does not *describe* what is. It *evokes* to being what is not until it has been spoken. This kind of speech resists discipline, shuns precision, delights in ambiguity, is profoundly creative, and is itself an exercise in freedom. In using speech in this way, we are in fact doing in a derivative way what God has done in the creation narratives of Genesis. We are calling into being that which does not yet exist (cf. Rom. 4:17).

Now in contrasting these two kinds of language, we need to be clear about the social function of each. The first mode of language—appropriate to science, engineering, and perhaps the social sciences—when used in the arena of human interaction, tends to be conservative, restrictive, limiting. It can only describe what already exists and, by its very use, deter anything new from coming into being. It crushes hope, for it cannot "imagine" what is not already present. By contrast, the bold, symbolic use of language in the Psalms is restive with what is. It races on ahead to form something new that never was before. This language then, with its speech of liberation, is dangerous and revolutionary, for its very use constitutes a threat to the way things have been. It is for that reason that totalitarian regimes, even when they control all the hardware, are most fearful of the poet. The creative speech of the poet can evoke new forms of human life which even the power of arms and repression is helpless to prevent. Such speech, which is the proper idiom for prayer, is the language of surprise. It means that in such speech both the speaker and God may be surprised by what is freshly offered. The language of the Psalms permits us to be boldly *anticipatory* about what may be, as well as *discerning* about what has been.

A great danger in praying the Psalms is that we shall mistakenly take their language in a positivistic, descriptive way as nothing more than a report on what is. Taken that way, the Psalms can probably be managed and comprehended and rendered powerless. That is a hazard of the repeated use of any important words. We assume we already know what they mean. But if the language of the Psalms is understood impressionistically and creatively, then it holds surprise and in fact creates new realities where none existed before.

Lament as Candor and Anticipation

Let us consider the function and power of such speech with reference to the two kinds of Psalms we identified in chapter 1. First, we said that *Psalms of lament are powerful expressions of the experience of disorientation.* They express the pain, grief, dismay, and anger that life is not good. (They also refuse to settle for things as they are, and so they assert hope.) One of the things to notice is that these Psalms engage in enormous hyperbole. Thus:

> I am poured out like water,
>   all my bones are out of joint,
>   my heart is like wax . . .
>   my strength is dried up like a potsherd (22:14-15).

> Every night I flood my bed with tears,
>   I drench my couch with my weeping (6:6).

> My tears have been my food day and night (42:3; cf. Isa. 16:9).

> My enemies trample upon me all the day long (56:1).

> I lie in the midst of lions (57:4).

What are we to make of this? If this be descriptive speech, we may take it as likely that not every bone is out of joint, that not the whole bed is drenched, that there must have been other meat, that the speaker has not been trampled all day, for that happens only in TV wrestling. Or if it is descriptive, we must conclude that the speech is irrelevant, because it resembles no experience of our own. But this is not descriptive language. It is evocative language used to create between speaker and God something that did not fully exist before, namely, a total, publicly acknowledged event of dislocation and disorientation. With this speech, the dislocation becomes a visible event that now exists between the pray-er and God. With this portrayal, God is compelled to notice. We now know, of course, that at the time of death, the healthy grief process requires many tears, many words, many embraces, many retellings of the grief. It is so for every extremity of dislocation. This is indeed grief *work* and we are invited to join in it.

The function of such lament speech is to create a situation that did not exist before the speech, to create an external event that matches the internal sensitivities. It is the work of such speech to give shape, power, visibility, authenticity to the experience. The speaker now says, "It is really like that. That is my situation." The listener knows, "Now I understand fully your actual situation in which you are at work dying to the old equilibrium that is slipping from you." The language may even run ahead of the event. Ricoeur[1] (to whom much of this discussion is indebted), following Freud, has seen that the authentic artist is not focusing on old events for review (after the manner of the analyst) but is in fact committing an act of hope. Art therapists know that persons who draw and paint are not simply announcing the old death but are choosing a future they are yet to embrace. Thus the lament Psalms of disorientation do their work of helping people to die completely to the old situation, the old possibility, the old false hopes, the old lines of defense and pretense, to say as dramatically as possible, "That is all over now."

When we hear someone speak desperately about a situation, our wont is to rush in and reassure that it is not all that bad. And in hearing these Psalms, our natural, fearful yearning is to tone down the hyperbole, to deny it for ourselves and protect others from it because it is too harsh and, in any case, is an overstatement. And likely we wish to hold on a bit to the old orientation now in such disarray. Our tendency to such protectiveness is evident in the way churches ignore or "edit" these "unacceptable" Psalms.

Our retreat from the poignant language of such a Psalm is in fact a denial of the disorientation and a yearning to hold on to the old orientation that is in reality dead. Thus an evangelical understanding of reality affirms that the old is passing away, that God is bringing in a newness (2 Cor. 5:17). But we know also that there is no newness unless and until there is a serious death of the old (cf. John 12:25, 1 Cor. 15:36). Thus the lament Psalms of disorientation can be understood, not in a theoretical but in a quite concrete way as an act of putting off the old humanity that the new may come (cf. Eph. 4:22-24).

So how pray these Psalms? I suggest that praying them requires the location of experiences in our own lives and in the lives of others, when such inclinations and realities of disorientations were singing among us. The events of a bed full of tears, of a body full of disconnectedness, of a plate full of salty tears, of a day full of trampling—these are events not remote from us. In our disciplined, restrained ways of managing, we may be too uptight to cry so. We may be too dulled to feel the trampling or to acknowledge it. But we do know what it feels like to be kicked when we are down. How wondrous that these Psalms make it clear that precisely such dimensions of our life are the stuff of prayer. The Psalms thus become a voice for the dying in which we are all engaged, partly because the world is a place of death and is passing away, partly because God gives new life, but only in the pain of death. It is because God is at work even in the pain of such death that the Psalmist dares enter God's presence with these realities. They have to do with God.

Language Permitting Transformation

The *celebrative Psalms of thanksgiving and hymns powerfully express experiences of reorientation.* The reorientation is always a surprise and a gift. It always comes to us just when we thought it not possible, when we could not see how it could be wrought in the present circumstance. The reorientation is not an achievement coming from us. It is not an automatic "next stage" ordained in our body, but it is something we receive when we did not expect it at all. Life falls into patterns of wholeness where we did not think it could happen precisely and only because God is at work.

Again we shall see that the Psalms of celebration also greatly overstate the case because they are essentially promissory. That is, they are not descriptions of what is evident, but they are renderings of what is surely promised and toward which the speaker is prepared to live. It may be urged, here more than in the Psalms of lament, that these statements engage in fantasy and assert things which are not "in hand." Thus, for example, the key assertion of these Psalms, "Yahweh is king," strikes one as ludicrous in our world, because most of the evidence of the newspapers suggests God is not in power. If the words must be descriptive, then such a claim is deceptive, for God manifestly is not king. But if the words are evocative of a new reality yet to come to being, then the words have a powerful function. And indeed, sometimes in a world where the circumstances are hopeless, then a promissory word is all that stands between us and the chaos. Then it is important to pray and speak and sing and share that word against all that data. For such a word stands like a barrier thrown up against the sea (cf. Jer. 5:22). And we do know that in our most precious friendships, sometimes there is only a word between us and misery, between us and death. But that word is not a fantasy. It is, rather, a precious gift on which we will stake everything. Thus as the Psalms of lament are acts of *painful relinquishment,*[2] so celebrative Psalms are acts of *radical hope.*

In the Psalms of celebration, we may consider three ways of speaking which correlate to those we have cited in the laments.

First, songs of lament focus frequently on the threat of enemies seeking to destroy. Many of these Psalms speak about *enemies*, even though they are not clearly identified. The responding assertion of celebration is that *Yahweh is king*, that God is graciously inclined and powerfully enthroned and that because of his rule, the enemies are no threat. Most scholars agree that at least in Pss. 47, 93, 96-99 this is the central motif. In a less precise way, this is a main theme of every song of celebration: the triumphant rule of Yahweh against every agent who would diminish us. Those who pray this kind of Psalm will want not just to reflect on a general notion of well-being but to work with the concrete image of king, the gracious ruler who does indeed manage well, provide for, protect the weak, and intervene for the helpless. To provide concreteness, it may be useful to focus in our own lives on situations when the presence of a trusted, respected person made a decisive difference, simply by being present. Or one may wish to reflect on the times of intervention when the kingship of Jesus totally redefined a situation (cf. Mark 3:1-6, 5:15, 5:41-42, 6:41-44).

Second, we have commented on the *diet of tears* that belongs to the lament. In the songs of celebration, the metaphor of tears is perhaps balanced by the metaphor of food, of banquet, of *a bounteous table*. Of course, the best known of these is in Ps. 23:5, "Thou preparest a table before me in the presence of my enemies." For a terser style, see Ps. 146:7, which relates food to those who are hungry and Ps. 147:9, food to the other creatures of the earth (cf. 81:10). An engagement of the metaphor of food is fundamental. There is no gesture as expressive of utter well-being as lavish food—as every Jewish and every Christian mother knows. Thus the feeding miracles of Jesus and the Eucharist are gestures of a new orientation which comes as surprising gift and ends all diets of tears.

Third, we have considered the metaphor of being *trampled* as a motif of disorientation. Notice that in being trampled, one is passive and acted upon. I suggest that in the songs of celebration, perhaps a counterpart of being trampled on is the act of *clapping*, of actively publicly engaging in a concrete gesture of commitment and reception of the new time. The clapping is to cheer the new king, i.e., the new orientation, the arrival of the promised kingdom (Pss. 47:1, 98:8; cf. Isa. 55:12). Less concrete, but related to it, is the call to praise; so that in the later Psalms (especially 148, but cf. 149:1-3,5-6), everything and everyone is mobilized to applaud, welcome, and receive. In praying these Psalms, the one who prays may want to recall times in which there was some good news which had to be shared. Other people had to be recruited to celebrate and rejoice because the news was too good to keep to one's self (cf. Luke 15:6,9,23).

Poetry Requiring Work

So let me conclude this with three comments. First, I have urged that the Psalms are filled with *metaphors* which need to be accepted as metaphors and not flattened into descriptive words. Metaphors are quite concrete words rooted in visible reality but yet are enormously elastic, giving full play to imagination in stretching and extending far beyond the concrete referent to touch all kinds of experience. The meaning of the metaphor is determined not only by what is there but by what we bring to it out of our experience and out of our imagination. The work of prayer is fully to explore and exploit the metaphor in terms of our own experience. Thus "table" does not mean simply what the speaker in Ps. 23 means, but it means all the good tables at which you have ever sat and the experiences of joy that happened there and the subsequent vibrations you have from them. "Tears night and day" does not refer simply to the crying a particular Psalmist did, but to all the times of crying in which you have engaged the death of the old world and all the times you have needed to cry but were unable to, all the bitterness and rejection which both caused crying and prevented it. All that is to be brought to the metaphor. Metaphors are not packaged announcements; they are receptive vehicles waiting for a whole world of experience that is itself waiting to come to expression. And if in the praying of the Psalms, we do not bring the dynamic of our own experience, we shall have flat, empty prayers treating the language as one-dimensional description.

Second, this exposition assumes something about how we read and study and hear these materials. The Psalms do not insist that we follow word for word and line by line, but they intend us to have great freedom to engage our imagination toward the Holy God. Our listening mostly moves in and out by a free association of ideas. Whether we plan it or not, are permitted or not, we will take liberties as the Psalm passes by to move out into the richness of our experience and then back into the awesome presence of God. That is the way of metaphors. They are not aisles down which we must move; they are more like rockets which explode in ways we cannot predict, causing some things to become unglued and creating new configurations of sensitivity. Like other rockets, if we are attentive they may both shatter and illuminate. The Psalms are our partners in prayer. Such evocative language permits both partners a marvelous freedom with which to surprise the other.

Third, I have offered three pairs of metaphors which I suggest can be useful in bringing experience to the Psalms:

> *enemies who destroy | king who orders and governs*
> *being trampled | clapping*
> *tears | table.*

The first element of each pair comes from the laments. The speech and experience of disorientation is a sense of being gotten at and trampled which reduces to tears. The second triad is for celebration: of having a sense of all-rightness, of needing to dramatize it, and of knowing nourishment. With such a simple scheme, many of the Psalms are embraced and much of our experience is submitted.

The images and metaphors I have suggested are rather at random. The Psalms are rich with others. And if these are not the ones that permit linkage for you, it will be easy enough to find others. If we do our proper work, we discover that these poetic pilgrimages are indeed ones with God "from whom no secret can be hid." In any case, this kind of language is not flat, obvious, or easy. It is language that requires us to work to bring something to it of our experience. But it also gives freedom. And when we speak this way, we are surprised by gifts given and lives raised from death.

Notes

1. Paul Ricoeur, *Freud and Philosophy* (New Haven: Yale University Press, 1970), pp. 165-177. Ricoeur increasingly seeks a hermeneutic of anticipation, which draws his work into relation with that of Jürgen Habermas.

2. On the lament as the route to hope, see Erhard Gerstenberger, "Der klagende Mensch," in *Probleme biblischer Theologie*, ed. Hans Walter Wolff (München: Chr. Kaiser Verlag, 1971), pp. 64-72; and W. Brueggemann, "The Formfulness of Grief," *Interpretation* 31 (1977): 263-275.

Chapter 3:

Language Appropriate to a Place

In our past chapter, we referred to "the liberation of language." That is the theme we intend to pursue here. It is our argument that the linkage between the Psalms and our experience requires understanding of and being attentive to language. The movement and meeting of God with us is indeed a speech-event in which new humanness is evoked among us. Being attentive to language means cultivating the candid imagination to bring our own experience to the Psalms and permitting it to be disciplined by the speech of the Psalms. And, conversely, it means letting the Psalms address us and having that language reshape our sensitivities and fill our minds with new pictures and images that may redirect our lives.

The notion of the "liberation of language" cuts two ways. On the one hand, we may be more free with our language, to let our language be liberated, not by being permissive or vulgar, but by letting it move beyond descriptive functions to evocative, creative functions in our life. That language should be free means we will turn it loose to form new possibilities for us—allowing us to engage in speech that is hope-filled.

On the other hand, the notion of the liberation of language is not only about *free speech,* but about *speech freeing us.* Thus we may become aware that when speech is broken free from a need for exactitude and permitted to reshape our existence and experience, we will experience new freedom that is not just freedom of speech, but freedom for faith.

Language matters enormously. If our speech and the speech of the Bible must be too closely managed, it likely means restriction both of God and us. On the other hand, free speech for God may release the energy which leads to "all things new."

The Psalmic metaphors we consider offer to us not descriptions but *news*, not situations but movements of God that will change things. Praying the Psalms means openness to God's pilgrimage toward us.

Our work in praying the Psalms is somehow to bring *the stylized, disciplined speech* of the Psalms together with the *raw, ragged, mostly formless experience* in our lives. We have suggested that a way to do this is by exploration and exploitation of metaphors, i.e., words that have concrete reference but which are open to remarkable stretching in many directions in order to touch our experience. The liberation of language means, then, that these words are free to work in many directions, but always without losing contact with their initial concreteness. And as words are used with such freedom, they function evocatively to shape and power our experience in new ways.

Being "In Place" and Displaced

I want now to focus on one specific pair of metaphors which speak of *place*. Paul Tournier has characterized the language of disorientation and reorientation in terms of (1) *finding* one's place and (2) *leaving* one's place for another.[1] The drama of disorientation and reorientation is as old in the Bible as the call to Abraham and Sarah to leave their place and go to another (Gen. 12:1). It is as pertinent as Jesus calling to the disciples to leave everything and to follow him (Mark 1:16-20, 10:28).

I do not suggest that these particular metaphors and images are any more important than others might be. But I pursue them as suggestive of the imaginative work of linkage that must be done in the praying of the Psalms.

The image of place in the Psalms suggests that in different *places* one prays different prayers. There are specific kinds of language appropriate to the situation in which one finds one's self. Speech about place is speech which enables both parties, speaker and God, to be clear about the nature of the interaction. The well-known Shaker song has it,

> 'Tis a gift to be simple,
> 'tis a gift to be free,
> 'tis a gift to come down
> where you ought to be.

We shall explore two images of place, one which finds Israel finally where it ought to be, the other which finds Israel in the utterly wrong place.

The "Pit" as the Wrong Place

The speech of the wrong place is, of course, found in the prayers of disorientation. In the laments, there is a great deal of talk about the *pit*. First, we know that the pit has concrete reality as a place in which to put people to render them null and void. In the pit, people are effectively removed from life. Historically, this is the device used for Joseph by his brothers (Gen. 37:22,28) and for the prophet Jeremiah by his enemies (Jer. 38:6-9). The pit is used against enemies. It means to deny to a person all the resources necessary for life. It is therefore not difficult to see how the specific reference became an embracive symbol for death. The pit reduces one to powerlessness.

It is of course difficult in the Psalms, as in any powerful poetry, to know when a word is being used descriptively and when it is being used metaphorically. But that is the power of this language. It always can have both tendencies. And it is probable that even the speaker was not always clear which way the word should be taken. That is why we may return again and again to these words. Each time we bring something different. And each time we find the Psalms' words shaped and nuanced in fresh ways.

Thus pit refers to the experience of being rendered powerless. In 28:1, to "be like those who go to the Pit," means to be silent, forgotten, dead. This is clearly a cry of disorientation, for the speaker fears losing the old relation with Yahweh, knowing then that everything is lost. In Ps. 88, the language is fuller. The speaker is characterized (vv. 4-5) as having no strength and as being forsaken, among the dead, slain, not remembered, cut off. The image evokes a torrent of words. The image is repeated in v. 6, expressed as dark and deep; and in v. 7, there is reference to the flood waters of chaos that will overwhelm. Thus the image tends to slide easily over into another one. If we were to use psychological language in the consideration of this Psalm, perhaps we would regard this as "severe depression." But the imagery of the Psalm cuts underneath psychology to talk about the multi-faceted experience involved. The poets are powerful in being able to bring such a struggle to visibility and concreteness. Notice that even though there is great detail, one cannot determine from the Psalm what the actual problem is— whether sickness, abandonment, guilt, imprisonment. The poet has an amazing capacity to say much and yet leave everything open. Thus the Psalm provides a marvelous receptacle which we are free to fill with our particular experience.

A different word, but with the same effect, is used in Ps. 30:9 which asserts that the pit is a place cut off from God so that God may neither help nor be praised there. In 35:7, there is a statement of attack against enemies who prepared the pit, so that dislocation may bring about a turning to God not only for vindication but for vengeance.

The cry for vengeance is a powerful part of disorientation. Such a cry blames those who have disrupted and demolished the old equilibrium. Thus in addition to the yearning to be *saved from* the pit, there is the counter-theme of wishing others would be *sent there*. There is nothing pious or "Christian" about this prayer. But (as psychotherapists know), our deep disorientation is not a time when we are able to be genuinely humane toward others because we are singularly attentive to the lack of humanness in our own life.

Thus there is the wish that the ones who have created the pit should be in it (9:15, cf. 94:13). In addition to the concrete word for *pit*, there is use of the word *Sheol*. This word has been mistakenly translated "hell." It does not refer to anything like that, for classical Israelite thought did not envision a place of ultimate punishment. Rather, the term refers simply to a place of undifferentiated, powerless, gray existence where one is removed from joy, and discourse with God. There is the wish that the troublemakers should go there (31:17, 55:16, 141:7).

Most remarkably, the dark, discouraging, deathly image of pit (cistern, ruin, Sheol) is used not only to describe a hopeless situation and to offer a counter-wish of the same for one's enemies. The image suggests also that there is real movement in its use. Those who stay with the image are able to speak not only in *prospect* of the pit or in the *midst* of trouble, but also *after* the trouble, in a mood of joy. The image occurs not only in songs of disorientation but in Psalms of thanksgiving which sing of reorientation:

> O Lord, thou hast brought up my soul from *Sheol*,
> restored me to life from among those gone down to the *Pit* (30:3).

> He drew me up from the desolate *pit*,
> out of the *miry bog* (40:2).

> For thou dost not give me up to *Sheol*,
> or let thy godly one see the *Pit* (16:10).

> Thou hast delivered my soul from the *depths of Sheol* (86:13).

We may note one other use which is of interest. The same motif is used in the song of thanksgiving in Jonah 2:2. In its present context, the reference purports to refer to the experience in the fish, but clearly the Psalm itself has an independent existence. Thus the reference to Sheol in v. 2 and pit in v. 6 can be filled with various content, depending on the circumstance of the speaker.

It is clear that the metaphor reports movement, first the cry of *anguish* about the pit, second the cry of *vengeance,* and third the voice of *thanksgiving.* The image permits the speaker to stay with the experience and see it through. The motif of pit enables the speaker to present every posture of life to God. Clearly the metaphor of pit in itself is of no interest to the Psalms, but it is a way of bringing life to God to have it dealt with.

So we have considered the concrete and metaphorical uses. Now, third, it remains that the contemporary user of the Psalms should take the image of pit and locate those experiences and dimensions of one's own life which are "the pits." This may include powerlessness, being abandoned, forgotten, lonely, helpless, cheated. It may be something as concrete as remembering being "stood in the corner" at school. Or it may be as powerful as a black person being made to "stay in his place," or a woman oppressed all this time by finding her only place to be the kitchen. Such occurrences in our lives can, with the help of the Psalms, be given concrete expression, and we can begin the process of moving past them— perhaps even to a song of celebration and thanksgiving. These Psalms attest to us that the life of faith does not protect us from the pit. Rather, the power of God brings us out of the pit to new life which is not the same as pre-pit existence. When one is in the pit, one cannot believe or imagine that good can come again. For that reason, the Psalmist finally focuses not on the pit but on the One who rules there and everywhere. It is the reality of God which makes clear that the pit is not the place "where you ought to be."

Under Safe Wings

Let us consider, in an abrupt transition, a second figure for *place* which is in every way contrasted with the first. A favorite image of Israel for a safe place with God is to speak of being safe under *the protective wings of God*. Whereas *pit* speaks of danger and threat, *wings* speak of safety, tenderness, and nurture. There is no doubt that the image is consciously derived from the concrete observation of how little birds are safe under the protective wing of the mother hen (cf. Deut. 32:11, Matt. 23:37, Luke 13:34).

But obviously the concrete reference becomes a metaphor which is much used in the songs of lament. It is a figure which yearns for safety, well-being, communion with God, or—in our language—a new orientation.

> Keep me as the apple of thy eye;
> hide me in the *shadow of thy wings* (17:8).

> Be merciful to me, O God . . . for in thee my soul takes refuge,
> in the *shadow of thy wings* I will take refuge (57:1).

Now it may occur to some that this image is an image of dependency in which one engages in a religious cop-out from the realities of life. That is a possible reading. But the image does not need to be understood as escapism. It may rather be discerned as evangelical realism, acknowledging that the resources for life are not found in "us" but will have to come from another source outside of self. It is the recognition of the disoriented person that a new orientation must come as a gift. Thus the metaphor embodies an openness to a new purpose, a submission to the will of another, a complete reliance upon the protective concern of another.

The two images, *protective wing* and *refuge* (which is of the genre of fortress and thus a war image) occur together in the lament of 61:2a-4:

Lead thou me
   to the *rock* that is higher than I;
for thou art my *refuge*,
   a *strong tower* against the enemy.
Let me dwell in thy *tent* for ever!
   Oh to be safe under the *shelter of thy wings!*

Notice here the cluster of images to which are added tent, rock, and tower, all used together to contrast with the current situation of need.

As with pit, so these images are not confined to situations of distress. And therefore they occur not only in the laments, but also in speeches of confidence and trust, rather as conclusions drawn from long experience. These are the voices of the reoriented:

The children of men take *refuge* in the *shadow of thy wings* (36:7).

You would confound the plans of the poor, but the Lord is his *refuge* (14:6; cf. 46:1).

These statements have the effect of vetoing the claim of the pit, of denying the pit the capacity to terrorize completely. They assert not that God will be or has promised to be a refuge, but that God *is* refuge right in the present circumstance. And therefore the words serve to redefine radically the place of the pray-er. He is verbally transported *from the pit to the wing, from the place of powerlessness to utter safety,* i.e., *from death to life.* And this change happens in the bold, free play of evocative language.

Our two positive images occur together in a remarkable Psalm of trust:

He who dwells in the *shelter* of the most high,
   who abides in the shadow of the Almighty,
will say to the Lord, my *refuge* and my fortress,
   my God in whom I trust . . .
Because you have made the Lord your refuge . . .
   no evil shall befall you . . . (91:1-2,9).

The capacity to speak the Psalms in the full freedom of imagination is already the embrace of a new orientation, an entry into the kingdom of God. It is of course possible that the words outdistance the realities. They could be spoken when an observer might conclude that the person is still in fact in the pit. But we live in pursuit of our imagination. Thus the use of the Psalm of trust while still in the pit is an act of profound hope which permits new life. Expressing one's trust in God's sheltering wings is a bold assertion that the power of the pit has been broken. Imaginative speech may outdistance actual circumstance. But it is a first gesturing of transformed circumstance.

This Psalm (91) is a remarkable convergence of motifs. In addition to our two images, it offers a variety of war images (vv. 4-8) which can usefully be explored and exploited. It offers animal imagery in v. 13 and speaks in v. 11 that marvelous offer, "He will give his angels charge of you." It concludes in vv. 14-16 with one of those rare responses of God which utterly transform. The self-assertion of God is a response to the boldness of submission:

I will deliver
I will protect
I will answer
I will be with
I will rescue
I will honor
I will satisfy
I will show

Finally concerning this metaphor, we should mention its surprising use in Ruth 2:12, where it is used in a narrative. Here, in communication on a human plane, the same image transforms a social situation.

In the Move from Pit to Wing

Our lives always move between *the pit* and *the wing,* between the shattering of disorientation and the gift of life. That is what our baptism is about, to die and to rise with him to newness of life (Rom. 6:1-11).

It remains for the user of this metaphor, like every other, to identify those events and experiences in which hovering wings have cared, in which we have been made utterly safe and so free that life has begun again. Every man, woman, and child of us has been within and shall again face the pit, and this must be brought to speech. Every one of us has the wings assured to us (cf. Deut. 33:27), and that also must be spoken about.

It is clear that the Psalms, when we freely engage ourselves with them, are indeed subversive literature. They break things loose. They disrupt and question. Most of all, they give us new eyes to see and new tongues to speak. And therefore, we need not enter the Presence of the Holy One mute and immobilized. We go there to practice our vocation of receiving the new future God is speaking to us. To risk such prayer is to repent of the old orientation to which we no longer belong. It is to refuse the pit which must first be fully experienced for the sake of the wings which may be boldly anticipated.

Notes

1. Paul Tournier, *A Place for You* (New York: Harper and Row, 1968).

Chapter 4:

Christians in "Jewish Territory"

The Psalms are a centerpiece of Christian liturgy, piety, and spirituality. They have been so from the beginning of the Christian movement for good reason. They have been found poignant in expression, able to empower believing imagination in remarkable ways. This is evident in the rich use made of the Psalms through the New Testament, most especially in the passion of Jesus. But the use of the Psalms by Christians is not without awkwardness, for the Psalms are relentlessly Jewish in their mode of expression and in their faith claims. And with our best intent for generosity and good faith, the different nuances of Jewish and Christian faith are not to be overlooked or easily accommodated.

Christian Modes of Avoidance

Two characteristic ways of handling this issue in the Psalms are easily identifiable. The first way is to be *highly selective* and make use of those Psalms which are most congenial to us and which contain the least objectionable "Jewishness." We may do this by completely avoiding some Psalms, e.g., Ps. 109, because it is too full of rancor and venom, or Ps. 137, which too harshly expresses its passion for brutal retaliation. These, it would seem at first glance, have no acceptable place in "conventional Christian faith." Or we may make our selection more delicately and only screen out certain verses. Thus for example, in Ps. 145, a marvelous statement of trust, v. 20b comes as a shattering negative at the end and is usually left off. Or Ps. 95:1-7a is a much used call to worship. But vv. 7b-11 are judged excessively concrete and negative—even though the writer of Heb. 3:7-11, 4:3-11 found these verses pertinent in an appeal for Christian fidelity. We may make our selections on grounds other than those used by the New Testament.

But note, we have spoken about "conventional Christian faith." There is, to be sure, a broad body of the Psalms which is unobjectionable in this regard. They move in a much broader, more irenic pattern of rhetoric. They speak in a way that lends itself to any serious religious commitment without being excessively concrete. Sensitivity to "Jewish awkwardness" has led much Christian practice to stay on this "safe" ground. But obviously that is to avoid and not confront the question we seek to face here.

The other characteristic way (not unrelated to the first) is to claim that Christianity, especially the New Testament, evolved from and is superior to the Old Testament Jewishness and thus *supersedes* it and can disregard "objectionable parts." On the one hand, this may lead us to imagine Christians have "outgrown" the offensive Jewishness of the Psalms and so legitimate the criteria for selectivity noted above. On the other hand, Jewish motifs are retained but "spiritualized." That is, they are taken to refer to matters other than the concrete referent. This may permit "christological" interpretation. Especially is this true of reference to "Jerusalem" (cf. 84:7, 122:6, 147:2) which may be taken to refer to Jesus, to a heavenly Jerusalem, only less concretely to any place of worship or meaning.

Again, a long-standing practice (going back to very early Christian interpretation) is to treat the Psalms as claims about Jesus Christ. In the tradition of Augustine, for example, there is a tendency to find hints about the life, ministry, death, and resurrection of Jesus at many points in the Psalms.

It is not easy to know how to assess such a practice. On

the one hand, it may seem to make the Psalms more readily available for Christian use. On the other hand, I suggest such "spiritualizing" tends to tone the Psalms down and avoid the abrasive and offensive elements. On balance, I believe it more helpful to avoid such a practice. We will be helped to a more genuine piety and an authentic faith if we engage the Psalms as poetry about our common, particular humanness. Nothing should be done which detracts from that reality. Facing such a "Christian" alternative, we should be more attentive to the rawness of Jewish faith out of which the Psalms speak.

But there is another alternative. It is in the prayers of Jesus that we may link Jewish ways of praying and christological interpretation. For the prayers of Jesus are surely prayers of a Jew. He prayed as a Jew. And the entire tradition of Christian prayer and Christian use of the Psalms must be seen in this light. This gives us warrant for christological interpretation, but the centrality of Jesus can never be far separated from the Jewish character of the material.

We are now, especially because of the holocaust, at a new place in Jewish-Christian conversations. Old presuppositions and behaviors will no longer do. We are at a new place where we must take each other with a new kind of seriousness, albeit with a new kind of awkwardness. It is clear that either *selectivity* or *spiritualizing* in fact simply avoids the resilient Jewishness of the Psalms. Moreover, our new situation makes clear that something urgent is at stake for us Christians in this question. It is clear that embrace of Jewishness in the Psalter must be faced not for the sake of the Jews, not out of respect because we are "persons of good will," not out of a notion of brotherhood. Rather, the Jewishness of the Psalms must be faced because our spirituality is diminished and trivialized if we neglect the Jewishness that belongs to our own tradition and practice of faith. It is for *our* sake and not the sake of the Jews that we are pressed to make this dimension of the Psalms our own. This is an exceedingly difficult and complex issue, not to be resolved here. Perhaps three aspects of the problem can provide a beginning both for our common prayer and for our educational tasks.

Praying for Jews

The Jewishness of the Psalms invites us to *pray for the Jews.* This is not meant to be a condescension, as though our prayers matter more than theirs. Nor does it mean praying for conversion of the Jews—the commonness of our faith precludes any such issue. Rather, it means to bring to utterance the deepest longings, echoes, and yearnings of the Jews, for Jews are a paradigm of the deepest longings and yearnings of all of humanity. And we dare say that in them we may hear even the profound sighs of the Almighty who must also practice something very Jewish in "his" day-to-day sojourn.

And for every brand of Jewishness (Zionist or not), these aches and yearnings have to do with Jerusalem. (See Luke 13:34-35, 19:41-44, where Jesus aches and groans over Jerusalem.) In the matrix of the holocaust and the modern state of Israel, both present yearnings and future hopes as well as remembered anguishes are linked to Jerusalem.

To pray for Jews is to recognize how pervasive is zeal for Zion in the Psalms. Externally, this may be so because the completed Psalter was undoubtedly shaped by priestly and/or political interests for whom Jerusalem is the center of the universe. Thus the Jerusalem interest has a tinge of ideology in the Psalms. It is true that Jerusalem has emerged as a gathering and focusing symbol for all of Israel's life. It embodies the memory of great political power under David and Solomon. It articulates the assurance of God's presence near his creation and among his folk (Isa. 4:2-6). It holds the promise of a world of justice and peace (Isa. 2:2-4). As Christians sing with another referent, so Jews may and must sing of Jerusalem.

"The hopes and fears of all the years are met in thee tonight." That carol which sings "tonight" is not very different from the formula from the night of the passover, "next year in Jerusalem"—the Jewish rendition of the biblical dream of justice, freedom, and well-being.

Thus after the entry into the Psalter by way of the Torah in Ps. 1, the Psalter moves to Zion in 2:6 and concludes at Zion in 149:2. With Jews, we can pray for the peace of Jerusalem (Ps. 122:6). With Jews, we may set Jerusalem above our highest joy (Ps. 137:6). With Zion, we are summoned to praise the Lord (147:12). Indeed, Ps. 128:5 suggests that Jerusalem is always on the tip of the tongue, even when the agenda is something else (cf. 2:6, 122:6, 147:12, 149:2). To be sure, we may know at the same time that *in the end time*, true worship is not "placed," but is in "spirit and in truth" (John 4:20-24). But *in the meantime*. . . . So there is a tension. We cannot leave Jerusalem as the flat, one-dimensional city of cynical Solomon. But also, we cannot run away from Jerusalem, for it embodies the meanings and the hopes, the fears and yearnings of our faith tradition. And we know that it also embodies the best yearnings of most of humanity. The reality of Jerusalem keeps alive among us the conviction that the world is not closed and fixed. Something more is promised. And for that we wait. Praying for Jews means the practice of a solidarity in concrete hope that is old and deep in our faith.

Praying with Jews

When we have *prayed for Jews*, by turning to Jewish shapes of reality, then in our use of the Psalms, we may perchance pray *with the Jews*. Our prayer life is always sorely tempted to individualism or at least to parochialism. We are urged by God's spirit to pray *along-side* and so to be genuinely ecumenical. As we use the Psalms, it is appropriate to ask *which Jews* have used these same Psalms with passion and at risk. And a parade of victims comes to our imagination. Or, with more immediacy, which Jews now pray these Psalms, from the frightened victims of anti-Semitism to the fated soldiers in the Israeli army, to the Jews in our own culture who are forever displaced and always at the brink of rejection and despisement. To pray with Jews is to be aware of the solidarity with the *chosen* of God whom the world *rejects*. To be sure, the Jews are an enigma, and we cannot ever identify that people by any simple category. But they stand as an odd testimony that God stands by and with and for those whom the world rejects.

To *pray with* introduces a fresh agenda into our Christian spirituality:

1) It tilts us toward a very specific history as *our history*. Thus see, for example, Pss. 78, 105, 106, 136, which provide a history of betrayal and disobedience, of surprise and deliverance. That history which becomes ours in prayer is a minority history, a history of victims and marginal people. But we need not romanticize. This history is also a memory of grasping and not trusting and thereby bringing trouble. That history may be a critique of our usual histories on which we count too heavily, a history of a triumphal church or an imperial nation or an intolerant culture. *Praying with* may lead us to another, converted identity.

2) Jews cannot pray very long without meditating on *the Torah* (Pss. 1, 19, 119). The Torah at the center of spirituality may deliver us from excessive romanticism or mysticism or subjectivity. Jewish preoccupation with the Torah is hard-nosed realism about the given norms of our life, about the ethical context of our faith, about the public character of true religion. The Torah at the center reminds us that the primal mode of faithfulness and knowing God is obedience. These Jewish prayers are affirming and joyous, celebrative of the realization that the Torah is not only command but assurance, not only a rule but a bulwark. Reality is structured in ways that will not be defeated. And power is given to share in this God-ordained structuring of reality. Life has a moral coher-

ence on which we can rely. That moral coherence (experienced as obedience) makes a difference to the keeping of God's promises.

3) To pray with Jews means to live with them in the hope and danger of *real judgment*. There is no doubt in the Psalter that God takes folks seriously. On the one hand, God takes folks seriously and lets us have what we choose (Pss. 1:4-6, 2:7, 50:16-18, 145:20). But on the other hand, the arena for spirituality is this: Jews know that this God who honors our ways is the same God who overrides our ways (Pss. 19:12-13, 103:8-14, 130:3-5). This tension lies at the heart of spirituality in the Psalms. The tension is that God gives us permission to choose our futures and, at the same time, God chooses a future for us that is gracious beyond our choosing. This tension must be lived with and not resolved. It must not be reduced to a scholastic problem of freedom and predestination. In each Psalm, each moment must be taken for itself and not yielded easily to some alternative claim or to some overarching scheme. The Jewish awkwardness with which we must contend concerns a *special history* as the elect ones, a *special claim* in the Torah which assumes and compels, and a *special awe* before the reality of God's judgment and mercy. To *pray with* Jews means to stay as long as these poems do at the raw edge with a live God who will not let us settle easily or for too long. There is a precariousness in this life of faith. Jews have known that for a very long time. Such prayer is risky because we have to do here with a God who is himself precarious and at risk. And the gift of the Jews in this literature is that we may be engaged with this very same God.

Praying as Jews

If we could genuinely pray *for Jews* and pray *with Jews*, then perhaps we can risk this presumption. (It is of course an enormously presumptuous thing for a Gentile to suggest, but we must not lose nerve in receiving the gift of these texts.) In the providence of God, we might be permitted (and required) to pray *as Jews.* I state the point with uneasiness. The uneasiness is of two kinds. First, it is impossible to identify Jewishness, and so it is too bold to say what it is to be "as Jews." Second, becoming a Jew takes many centuries and many generations. And I am under no romantic illusions about quick transformations. Few of us have lamented in Babylon or been close enough to the ovens when they have been heated. But given those admissions and misgivings, let us hint at five dimensions of Jewishness which mark the Psalms, dimensions that might matter to our spirituality.

I make no claim that these marks are essentially "Jewish." But I speak of them this way on two grounds. First, they seem to me to be facets of the Psalms which are most troublesome to us, which Christians most prefer to screen out as awkward and offensive. Second, even if they are not definitively Jewish, they at least stand in contrast to the dominant "Greek" reasonableness and idealism which have shaped our spirituality. What I have called "Jewish" at least contrasts with the cool, detached serenity (not to say apathy) of which we are inheritors (and too often practitioners).

1) The Psalms are awkward in their *concreteness.* They do not engage in sweeping generalizations to which we are observers. The imagery and speech is pointed and specific. This is true of the historical references to Zion, to king, to enemies. Psalmic rhetoric is concrete about commandments and punishments, about angers, loves, and hopes. Such a way of prayer may be a trouble when we want to pray "in general" without focusing anywhere. The "cultural despisers" of biblical faith consistently want a generalized religious consciousness and are offended by God become concrete. In Israel, this *scandal* is in God's way with the "nobodies." In the New Testament, the same *scandal* is in Jesus of Nazareth (Luke 7:22-23). The Psalms are "embodied" prayers.

2) There is no or little slippage between what is thought/

felt and what is said. The Psalms are *immediate*. There is no mediation to "clean up," censor, or filter what is going on. This directness reflects a readiness to risk in an uncalculating way with this one "from whom no secret can be hid." The Psalms dare to affirm that, as there are no secrets hid from God, so there likely is less self-deception at work in these prayers. These prayers are marked by *candor and robustness* with the God who "searches the heart" (Jer. 17:10, Prov. 20:27). These are the prayers of the liberated, who in their freedom are able to speak in an artistic way without ornamentation. Liberated prayer of this kind is filled with passion, i.e., with the conviction that in these words, something is at issue that can be resolved in more than one way. And which of the ways of resolution depends on how the prayer engages the person of God. There are not many evidences in the Psalms of depression, either psychological or spiritual. There are active passions such as rage, anger, and hatred, but this is contrasted with the immobility of depression. These Psalms in their candor are on the one hand sung because the singers have been liberated. On the other hand, these very songs are an act of emancipation. The songs both *reflect* and *accomplish* liberation. (It is no wonder that the therapeutic tradition of emancipation grows from this resilient and bold Jewish vision.) In the language of R. D. Laing, there is no split here between "experience" and "behavior."[1] What Israel *experiences* in the stuggle of faith is what it speaks in its *behavior* of the Psalms. In this identity of thought/feeling and speech, the Psalms overcome the calculating and careful distance that characterizes very much "polite" piety. Prayer stays very close to the realities of life in these poems.

3) The robustness and candor of the Psalms are especially evident in the *articulation of hatred and anger*. There is no thought here that Israel must be on good behavior in the presence of God. Everything at work in life is readily brought to expression. This prayer is an expression of "no more Mr. Nice Guy." Perhaps this freedom is birthed in the Exodus

event, in which Israel knows early that Pharaoh first must be identified as the enemy and then must be verbally assaulted. There is no courteous yearning for reconciliation here. Life is known to be conflicted. And therefore, the practice of conflicted and conflicting speech is necessary. Israel at prayer is ready to carry on linguistic assault against its enemies, one of whom is sometimes God. (Thus, it is not unimportant that Job, that most honest of pray-ers in Israel, is named "enemy." That is, the word *Job* means "enemy." Israel at prayer is prepared to speak as enemy.) Israel does not envision a false community in which unequal partners love each other in their unjust and unequal positions.

Well before Paul (Eph. 4:26), the Psalmists endorse the notion, "be angry but do not sin" (cf. Ps. 4:4). Anger is here in abundance. And anger is topped by hatred. The true believer hates powerfully and finds a community with Yahweh (the God of Israel) who also hates:

> Do I not hate them that hate thee, O Lord?
>   And do I not loathe them that rise up against thee?
> I hate them with perfect hatred;
>   I count them my enemies (Ps. 139:21-22).

Indeed, the speaker, like Yahweh, is never passive or apathetic. Of course it might be objected that the speaker too readily identifies his own hatred with that of God. Perhaps so. But in the moment of hatred, that is what happens to all of us. This anger is not only spiritually liberated. It is psychologically honest. It asserts what each of us in our moment of insane hatred tends to do. In that moment, we are incapable of maintaining critical distance from our own sensitivities.

God as well is one who is capable of hatred for evildoers (Pss. 5:5, 31:16). Our objection to the Psalms' expression of hatred reflects our notion that God is incapable of such a posture. But that is how it is with the God of the Psalms. Such a conviction about *God* permits this practice of *piety*.

And the rage goes even deeper. The rage born of anger

and hatred can be turned against God. In a no-holds-barred extremity, Job articulates venom even against God:

> Though I am innocent, my own mouth would condemn me;
>   though I am blameless, he would prove me perverse . . .
> It is all one; therefore I say, he destroys both the blameless
>   and the wicked (Job 9:20,22).

There is something peculiarly Jewish about such a posture that completely reidentifies both God and the speaker. Here is no "unmoved mover," no object to be adored, no "Ground of Being." Here is the Ultimate Partner who must enter the fray and be at issue along with the speaker. It should be clear that the Jewish interaction between the two, God and pray-er, is contrasted with our conventional piety. And we learn so slowly that such candid piety speaks to what is really at stake. Risky as it is, this piety makes a genuine, healing difference in life. And as such, it serves as an important model for human interaction as well.

4) But Israel is not able only to rage with abandon. Israel has equal *passion for hope*. Elie Weisel, that most remarkable story-teller from the holocaust, has said that what makes a Jew a Jew is this inability to quit hoping. Jewishness consists in "going on," in persisting, in hoping. Whatever be the psychological elements of hope, the structure of hope is the conviction of a new world. A new gift from God is at work on our behalf. And this new gift from God is at work, critiquing, dismantling, and transforming the present age which is so characterized by injustice and enmity. It is characteristically Jewish to hope for newness from God, from this specific God who is a giver of newness. Here is no fascination with "being." Even "nature" is understood as creation, called by God to bring forth newness (cf. Pss. 65:9-13, 145:13b-16). It will not do (as Westermann[2] and Terrien[3] have shown) to focus on historical events to the neglect of the structure and character of "nature." But "nature" as well (better "creation"), is not fixed and settled. It also lives under hope and will be

transformed for the new age. Thus Israel hopes for the structures of creation as well as for the specificity of human communities.

Following Westermann, Gerstenberger has seen that even the lament Psalms are acts of hope.[4] They articulate the deepest hurt, anger, and rage of Israel. But they are not statements of resignation which accept the bad situation. Rather, they are insistences upon and expectations from God, who can and will, may and must, keep promises. Many examples could be cited. With two different words, Ps. 71 presents this deep hope:

> For thou, O Lord, art my hope,
>   my trust, O Lord, from my youth (v. 5).

> But I will hope continually,
>   and I will praise thee yet more and more (v. 14).

Notice the hope is rooted in God, not in the situation. And hope is affirmed precisely in the face of mocking enemies (vv. 10-13).

5) The practice of concreteness and candor, of anger and hope, is carried out with exceeding passion in the Psalms. They prepare us for the most striking and problematic element of Jewish prayer, the *readiness to seek vengeance*. We will delay for now any extended discussion of the topic and take it up separately in the next chapter. For now we must do two things. First, we must recognize that vengeance is both central and problematic in the Psalms. Second, we must recognize that such a yearning for revenge occurs not in a vacuum, but precisely in the context of the qualities we have already presented as characteristically Jewish. The seeking of revenge should be expected from a people who *hate* and *hope* with such passion. A religion which practices *candor* and a piety which is *specific* will predictably give vent to the yearning for revenge.

As "Jews of Tomorrow"

Notice that these five elements which concern *praying as Jews* provide a critique of much Christian spirituality. Our suggestion is not that we simply observe these factors as interesting items in the Psalms. Rather, the Psalms are an invitation to transform our piety and liturgy in ways that will make both piety and liturgy somewhat risky and certainly abrasive. Lewis Mumford has written of the relentless Jewish resistance to every assimilation.[5] Jewishness, wherever it occurs, is an awkwardness to those who want to create a "universal culture," or a "preachable kingdom." The practice of Jewish piety maintains its odd angularity. And that angularity has dangerous public implications. Obviously a people so passionate in prayer will not willingly practice silent subservience in public life. A community so laden with visions of Torah will not be silent in the streets about injustice. Prayers *with* and *for* and *as* the people of Jerusalem will not long acquiesce in public violation of these visions.

Finally, a word in anticipation of response to these comments. Surely it will occur to some that such an insistence on Jewishness, and especially Jerusalem, is not very evenhanded toward the current political issues surrounding Israel and Jerusalem. My comments have important political implications, but not of that kind.

The theological claims I have made here for Jewishness cut in various ways concerning historical responsibility and political reality. There is a closed kind of Jewishness that can become politically totalitarian. Such a Jewishness is no doubt at work in the modern world, and no doubt one can find some warrant in the Psalms. But there is another kind of Jewishness in the Psalter. And it is to that *alternative Jewishness* that attention must be drawn. The tension we face in the Psalms (and everywhere in the Old Testament) is the tension between *largeness of vision* and *passion for particularity*. Thus far, we have focused on the passion for particularity because I judge that to be the stumbling block for many Christians who face the Psalms.

But largeness of vision is not antithetical to such a passion for particularity. It grows out of it. The *elect* people bear witness to an all-inclusive *providence*. So the counter-theme to Jewish particularity is a vision of all peoples who may also be citizens of Jerusalem (cf. Isa. 2:2-4, Rev. 21:1-4) or who may be reckoned as distinct from Israel but nonetheless part of the fulfillment of God's promise (Isa. 19:23-25).

1) The Psalms have a *passion for the righteous,* for the practitioners of God's vision for justice and peace (Pss. 1:5-6, 7:9, 11:7, 34:15, 92:12). And the Psalms are reluctant to equate this commitment with any narrow community. In its largeness of vision, Israel knows there are "Torah keepers" in various communities, some of which bear other names (Isa. 56:6-8).

2) The Psalms have a *passion for the poor and needy* (Pss. 69:33, 109:31, 140:12), for those broken of spirit and heart (Pss. 34:18, 51:17). God's compassion is not toward an ethnic community nor those with a pedigree, but toward those in special need.

These elements also belong to the Jewishness of the Psalter. Thus as one envisions the drama of Jerusalem and as those who yearn to be "next year in freedom," the pilgrimage to Jerusalem is a strange procession. That procession toward newness includes the Jews who bear a public identity, but it also includes refugees who are remote from the name "Jew." The Jewishness to which the Psalter calls us is not that of "yesterday's Jews" who rest on the faith of their parents (cf. Matt. 3:9), but on the "Jews of tomorrow" who dare to believe God's concrete promises with passion.

There is a strange restlessness and shattering that belongs to Jewishness. When we learn to pray these prayers faithfully, we shall all be scandalized. Thus I propose that, at the end, conventional notions of Jewishness are also placed in question. But that is only at the end, after we have learned the passion and the patience to pray *for* and *with* and *as* Jews.

Notes

1. R. D. Laing, *The Politics of Experience* (New York: Random House, 1967), esp. chap. 1.

2. Claus Westermann has most fully articulated this viewpoint in *What Does the Old Testament Say about God?* (Atlanta: John Knox Press, 1979), esp. chap. 3. His earlier succinct statement is, "Creation and History in the Old Testament," in *The Gospel and Human Destiny*, ed. Vilmos Vajta (Minneapolis: Augsburg Publishing House, 1971), pp. 11-38.

3. Samuel Terrien, *The Elusive Presence* (New York: Harper and Row, 1978).

4. See Gerstenberger's work previously cited herein (p. 36, note 2). For a contemporary explication of this insight, see E. S. Gerstenberger and W. Schrage, *Suffering* (Nashville: Abingdon Press), pp. 130-135.

5. Lewis Mumford, *The Myth of the Machine* (New York: Harcourt, Brace and World, 1966, 1967), pp. 232-233.

Chapter 5:

Vengeance:
Human and Divine

The most troublesome dimension of the Psalms is the agenda of vengeance. It may also be the most theologically poignant, as we hope to show. The cry for retaliation at one's enemies at least surprises us. We do not expect to find such a note in "religious" literature. And it may offend us. It does not fit very well in our usual notions of faith, piety, or spirituality. To some extent, we are prepared for it by our recognition (in the last chapter) that the Psalms reflect unabashed concreteness, candor, and passion. The Psalms explore the full gamut of human experience from rage to hope. Indeed, it would be very strange if such a robust spirituality lacked such a dimension of vengeance, for we would conclude that just at the crucial point, robustness had turned to cowardice and propriety. The vitality of the Psalms, if without a hunger for vengeance, would be a cop-out. But we need have no fear of that. There is no such failure of nerve, no backing down from this religion on the brink of stridency. Thus the expression of vengeance is not unnatural, unexpected, or inappropriate. But that in no way diminishes its problematic character.

The Reality of Vengeance

Let us begin with two acts of realism. First, *the yearning for vengeance is there in the Psalms*. It is there, without embarrassment, apology, or censor. Whatever we say on the subject must be linked to that undeniable fact. And we are not free to explain it away. If we are genuinely to pray the Psalms, we must try to understand what is happening in such acts of piety. Certainly no expurgated, "selective" version of the Psalms will do. For that is only to push the problem away. Such "selectivity" does not avoid the presence of the motif. Indeed, selective avoidance will cause us to miss the resources that we may find there.

And the counterpart, a second act of realism, is that *the yearning for vengeance is here, among us and within us* and with power. It is not only *there* in the Psalms but it is *here* in the human heart and the human community. When we know ourselves as well as the Psalter knows us, we recognize that we are creatures who wish for vengeance and retaliation. We wish in every way we can to be right and, if not right, at least stronger. Perhaps we do not engage in child abuse or spouse abuse, and we do not urge the death penalty (at least all of us do not). But in lesser ways, we assault verbally or we nurse affronts, waiting for their reversal and satisfaction. It could be that for some few, these passions are absent or that for more of us, they are absent on occasion. But we must not be so romantic as to imagine we have outgrown the eagerness for retaliation. While developmental psychology may discern other more positive yearnings as an ideal, theological realism cannot afford such deception. The real theological problem, I submit, is not that vengeance is *there* in the Psalms, but that it is *here* in our midst. And that it is there and here only reflects how attuned the Psalter is to what goes on among us. Thus, we may begin with a recognition of the acute correspondence between what is *written there* and what is *practiced here*. The Psalms do "tell it like it is" with us.

So let us begin with such *realism* about the poetry and about ourselves. The articulation of vengeance leads us to new awarenesses about ourselves. That is, the yearning for vengeance belongs to any serious understanding of human personality. It is important that it is in Psalm 139 that the *mystery of human personhood* is celebrated (vv. 1-2, 13-15); and it is the same Psalm that expresses the *capacity for hatred* (vv. 21-22). The capacity for hatred belongs to the mystery of personhood.

1) The Psalms are the rhetorical practice in fullest measure of *what is in us*. John Calvin describes the Psalms as "An Anatomy of all Parts of the Soul."[1] And so they are. They tell all about us. The Psalms provide space for full linguistic freedom in which nothing is censored or precluded. Thus Ps. 109 surely engages in "overkill" in its wishes and prayers against the "wicked." The words pile up like our nuclear stockpiles, without recognizing that nobody needs to be or could possibly be violated in that many ways. But this is not action. It is words, a flight of passion in imagination.

Such imagination, in which the speaker strains to be vivid and venomous and almost exhibitionist, surely performs several functions. (a) It is no doubt *cathartic*. We need not flinch from the therapeutic value of the Psalms. In our heavily censored society, this is one place left in which it may all be spoken. (b) But it is more than cathartic, more than simply giving expression to what we have felt and known all along. In genuine rage, words do not simply follow feelings. They lead them. It is speech which lets us discover the power, depth, and intensity of the hurt. The Psalms are acts of *self-discovery* that penetrate the facade of sweet graciousness. (c) The Psalms serve to *legitimate and affirm* these most intense elements of rage. In such speech, we discover that our words (and feelings) do not destroy the enemy, i.e., they are not as dangerous as we thought. Nor do our words bring judgment from heaven on us. The world (or God) is not as censorious as we feared. Such speech puts rage in perspective. Our feelings brought to speech are not as dangerous or as important as we imagined, as we wished, or as we feared. When they are unspoken, they loom too large, and we are condemned by them. When spoken, our intense thoughts and feelings are brought into a context in which they can be discerned differently. Notice that in Ps. 109, after the long recital of rage through v. 19, the intensity is spent. Then the speaker must return to the reality of heart and fear and helplessness in vv. 22-25. The rage is a prelude to the real agenda of attitudes about one's self.

2) It is important to recognize that these verbal assaults of imagination and hyperbole are *verbal*. They speak wishes and prayers. But the speaker doesn't *do* anything beyond speak. The *speech* of vengeance is not to be equated with *acts* of vengeance. This community which respected and greatly valued language encouraged speech, destructive as it might be, in the place of destructive action. So far as we know, even in the most violent cries for vengeance, no action is taken. These Psalms might help us reflect on retaliatory violence in a society which has lost its places and legitimacy for speech. Where there is no valued *speech of assault* for the powerless, the risks of *deathly action* are much higher from persons in despair.

3) The speech of vengeance is characteristically *offered to God*, not directly to the enemy. Thus Ps. 109 begins with an address to God. And in v. 21, the turn from venom to self-reflection happens in, "But Thou." The final appeal in v. 26 is no longer an urging to action but an imperative that God should act. That is, vengeance is transferred from the heart of the speaker to the heart of God. The Psalm characteristically is structured to show that vengeance is not simply a psychological but a theological matter. It must be referred to God. And when vengeance is entrusted to God, the speaker is relatively free from its power. The speaker, with all the hurt and joy, affirms himself/herself to be God's creature. That recognition of being in God's realm and able to address God gives perspective to the venom.

Thus the movement of the speech is in two parts. First, the vengeance must be *fully recognized* as present, *fully owned* as "my" rage, and *fully expressed* with as much power and intensity as possible. It must be given freedom for full play and visibility. It is analogous to grief. We know grief is best handled by full articulation. And Israel knows that same thing about rage.

But second, this full rage and bitterness is *yielded to God's wisdom and providential care.* This happens when the speaker finally says, "But thou."[2] The yielding cannot be full and free unless the articulation and owning is first full and freed. The yielding, i.e., submission to God, is an act of faith and confidence. The speaker has no doubt that God will honor and take seriously the need for vengeance and will act upon it. But the doxology of Ps. 109:30-31 makes clear that the final confidence is in God. It is not in the rightness of the venom or the legitimacy of the rage. There is no sense of being triumphant, but only of being very sure of God. By the end of such a Psalm, the cry for vengeance is not resolved. The rage is not removed. But it has been dramatically transformed by the double step of *owning* and *yielding.*

God's Vengeance and Our Vengeance

But such a prayer still shocks us. And it drives the issue one step further. *What about God?* What about this God who receives such prayers and at least leaves open the impression that "he"[3] shares the venom and will act on it. We need to begin by recognizing two things about God's self-presentation in the Psalms and in the entire Bible. First, there is no single, coherent picture of God. Nor is there a neat development from a vengeful to a loving God. Rather, there are various sketches and disclosures in different circumstances. Each such disclosure is offered on its own and makes its own claim. And each such sketch must be fully honored on its own without being reduced to a generalized portrait.

Second, every presentation of God is filtered through human imagination. The God presented in any sketch is not untouched by human interest, human need, and human wish. We can easily see that people with passionate hates assign these same hates to God. That is, we find it easy to identify our passions with the passions of God, and collapse the distance between us and the Holy One. But we must recognize that the "nice" presentations of God—as loving, forgiving, merciful—are also filtered through human interest, human need, and human wish.

So we may not easily take some disclosures of God as "more nearly true" simply because we happen to like them. The mystery, sovereignty, and freedom of God require us to hold loosely even our preferred sketches of God. And nowhere is this more important than in this question of vengeance. In these poems, we have an "interested," theological statement. But such a statement is not made without authenticity. That is, this is *serious* speech addressed to a *real* God, about things *genuinely important*. And our best theological treatment recognizes that these speeches may articulate our most important concerns to God. And we take these statements seriously only if we regard them as well-intended and deeply felt prayers.

1) The Psalms (and the entire Bible) are clear that *vengeance belongs to God* (Deut. 32:25, Ps. 94:1, Isa. 63:4, Rom. 12:19, Heb. 10:30). Vengeance is not human business. Now it may trouble us that this God is concerned with vengeance. But we may begin with the awareness that the assignment of vengeance to God means an end to human vengeance. It is a liberating assertion that I do not need to trouble myself with retaliation, for that is left safely in God's hands. The Psalmist seems to know that. The venomous words show that the reality of vengeance is present. But that these words are addressed to God shows a recognition that this is God's business and not ours. That is the first and most important thing to say about God's vengeance. To affirm that vengeance belongs to God is an act of profound faith. Conversely, to try to keep some vengeance for self and to withhold it from God is to mistrust God, as though we could do it better than God. Affirmation of God's vengeance is in fact a yielding.

2) The vengeance of God is understood as *the other side of his compassion*–the sovereign redress of a wrong. That is, in the Old Testament, two motifs belong together. God cannot act to liberate "his" people without at the same time *judging* and *punishing* the oppressors who have perverted a just ordering of life. Vengeance by God is not understood as an end in itself. It is discerned as necessary to the establishment and preservation of a just rule. It is a way God "right-wises" life. Thus Deut. 32:35 speaks of vengeance. But this is linked in v. 36 with vindication and compassion for "his" servants. Such a juxtaposition expresses political realism. When things are shifted on behalf of someone, it means a painful loss for someone else who has encroached on the claims of the first party. Such a juxtaposition may also reflect some childishness. When we are hurt, we do not feel the situation completely righted by compassion unless the offender is also dealt with. This understanding does not eliminate all the theological problems, but it is helpful to see that vengeance is the dark side, perhaps the inevitably dark side, of the mercy of God. Thus:

> . . . to him who smote the first-born of Egypt,
>   for his steadfast love endures forever . . .
> to him who smote great kings,
>   for his steadfast love endures forever (Ps. 136:10,17).

The killing of the first-born does not sound like "steadfast love," and it was not so perceived by any Egyptian. But that is steadfast love if one is an Israelite. And such an action is necessary to liberate, though from another perspective, it is simply ruthless vengeance.

3) That God practices vengeance is one way the Bible has of speaking about *moral coherence and moral order* in which God is actively engaged. The God of the Bible is never neutral, objective, indifferent, or simply balancing things. The world is not on its own. There is an accountability to the purposes of God to which all must answer. God who saves

and creates watches over "his" will and judges those who violate "his" purposes. Thus the God who *keeps loyalty* for thousands is also the one who *visits iniquities* to the fourth generation (Ex. 34:6-7). And "his" judgment is especially turned against the "wicked," i.e., those who do not serve "his" sovereign purpose (cf. Ps. 58:10, 149:7). The passionate appeal for faithfulness in Heb. 10 ends with such an affirmation:

> For we know him who said, "Vengeance is mine, I will repay." And again, "The Lord will judge his people." It is a fearful thing to fall into the hands of the living God" (vv. 30-31).

Such heavy imagery may not suit our tastes. But it is the imagery found most compelling in terms of urgency in the Church (cf. Luke 21:22). It may surprise some to note these anticipations of vengeance even in the New Testament.

4) The reality of *juxtaposition* (vengeance is the back side of compassion) and the *assurance of moral coherence* in which God has a stake (i.e., God takes human action seriously in terms of "his" purpose) leads to the affirmation that *God has taken sides in history* and acts effectively on behalf of "his" special partners. In the beginning, that special partner is Israel. And so "his" compassion is for Israel, "his" vengeance is against the enemies of Israel. And that is why there is the balance of the *rescue* of Israel and the *destruction* of others, as in Ps. 136:10,15,17-20. But Israel never becomes the possessor of God's compassion, nor the manager of God's vengeance. Both belong peculiarly to God. God alone exercises them in "his" sovereign freedom and for the sake of that sovereign freedom. When Job's friends, for example, imagine they can "administer" God's compassion, they are dismissed as "foolish."

Thus, in the long run the benefactor of God's compassion/vengeance is not Israel in any mechanical way. Rather, God's action is taken (a) on behalf of the *faithful* (i.e., righteous, obedient), those who keep Torah:

The righteous will rejoice when he sees the vengeance; he will bathe
his feet in the blood of the wicked.
Men will say, "Surely there is a reward for the righteous; surely there
is a God who judges on earth" (Ps. 58:10-11; cf. Ex. 34:6).

And God's action is taken (b) on behalf of the *poor and needy*
who are objects of "his" special concern:

Say to those who are of a fearful heart,
   "Be strong, fear not!
Behold our God will come with *vengeance*,
   with the recompense of God.
He will come and save you.
Then the eyes of the blind shall be opened,
   and the ears of the deaf unstopped;
Then shall the lame man leap like a hart,
   and the tongue of the dumb sing for joy" (Isa. 35:4-6).

. . . to bring good tidings to the afflicted . . .
   to proclaim liberty to the captives . . .
to proclaim the year of the Lord's favor,
   and the day of *vengeance* of our God (Isa. 61:1-2).

O Lord, thou God of *vengeance*,
   thou God of *vengeance*, shine forth! . . .
O Lord, how long shall the wicked,
   how long shall the wicked exult? . . .
They slay the widow and the sojourner,
   and murder the fatherless (Ps. 94:1,3,6; cf. 9:18, 12:5-7, 34:6, 35:10).

It is evident that this motif of *vengeance for the poor* is carried
into the New Testament, especially in the gospel of Luke. It is
articulated in the song of Mary (Luke 1:51-53) and in the
inaugural presentation of Jesus (Luke 4:18-19) which quotes
Isa. 62:1-2. The day of God's vengeance is the day of reversals[4]
for the poor and against the unjust rich.

The vengeance of God is not indiscriminate anger. It is a
reflection of God's zeal for "his" purposes of justice and
freedom. God will not quit until "he" has "his" way, which is
at odds with the ways of the world (cf. Isa. 55:6-9). And when
God's way is thwarted, say the Psalms, God powerfully intervenes—that is, the God with whom we have to do in this
practice of Psalmic spirituality.

There is no doubt that many of the uses of the vengeance motif in the Psalms are a mixture of *good theology* and *self-interested plea*. The speaker identifies himself/herself as one of the faithful deserving poor who has a right to expect and insist upon God's compassionate/vengeful intervention (cf. Ps. 40:17, 69:29).

This is most poignantly expressed in the "confessions" of Jeremiah. Jeremiah regards himself as undoubtedly one of the faithful poor who asks for *compassion* which must come as *vengeance* (cf. Jer. 11:20, 20:12). With Jeremiah, as with the Psalmists and with us, there are no disinterested pray-ers. But the Psalmists are bold to see an appropriate linkage between *God's primal commitment* and *our situation of need*. God's commitment is invoked because of a situation of distress that God does not will. And so God is summoned to intervene and to *invert* the situation. It is that appropriate linkage which is expressed in these Psalms. Such prayer is offered but not because of reasoned conclusion. Rather, in the hurt, anger, and shame, the point of contact is on the one hand the overwhelming need and, on the other, the awareness that Yahweh, God of Israel, is all we have. In that moment of need, Israel's God is the last, best hope of the believing community. And so Israel must seek *rectification*,[5] and that requires forceful action.

Vengeance and Compassion

Having said all of that, we may note that this settlement of the question of vengeance is provisional. The most sensitive poets of Israel are troubled about this way of thinking. And at peak moments of literary insight and theological imagination, they know God to be troubled too.

In the Old Testament, we may cite two texts, parallel in structure, which disclose the struggle in the heart of God. In the flood narrative, the beginning in Gen. 6:5-7 has God resolve to take vengeance on "his" wayward creation. But note that God makes the resolve not in anger, but in *grief and sorrow.* The flood narrative spins out the troubled tale. But by 8:21, something decisive has happened. Nothing is changed in the imagination of humankind, which is still evil. What has happened is a change wrought in the heart of God, who will no longer take vengeance. The move in God's heart from 6:5-7 to 8:21 suggests that instead of humankind suffering, God takes the suffering as "his" own. God resolves to turn the grief in on "himself" rather than to rage against "his" creation. God bears the *vengeance* of God in order that "his" creation can have compassion.

The same "turn" is more visible in Hos. 11:1-9. Verses 1-7 are a conventional statement of God's anger and punishment. But in vv. 8-9, God has internalized the rage, turned the anger so that "his" own "heart quakes." God resolves not to take vengeance on Israel, but to contain it within "his" own person. In this profound moment, God breaks with the habits of heaven and earth. God presents "himself" in radical graciousness. "He" is "God and not man." This God is also a God unlike any of the other gods (cf. Ps. 82). Such graciousness is not easy, in heaven or on earth. It is not simply or obviously gained. It is gained only by God's acceptance and internalization of the vengeance which gets outwardly expressed, now, only as compassion. Unmitigated compassion is possible only because God bears the pain of vengeance in "his" own person.

A Way Through Vengeance

Finally, we must ask, how does *Christian faith assess* these statements about the vengeance of God? How are these themes taken up in the New Testament? There is ground for saying that the New Testament discloses God as having moved from vengeance to compassion. But that argument must be articulated very delicately:

1) We must not pretend that the New Testament gives a "higher" view of God in contrast to the Old Testament. Such an evolutionary notion misreads the evidence. In both Testaments, we have to do with the same God.

2) We have seen that the Old Testament already knows about the problem in the experience of God's vengeance. Israel already understands that the grief of God moves beyond vengeance. In addition to Gen. 6:5-7, 8:20-22, and Hos. 11:8-9, which we have cited, see Pss. 103:6-14 and 130.

3) We have seen that the New Testament still makes important use of the motif of God's vengeance. In the New Testament, this God has not become a romantic who has no passion for "his" purposes. This God still holds to "his" jealous sovereignty and intervenes for the sake of it. There is no way around the hard sayings in the New Testament.

4) But, finally, we come to those staggering ethical injunctions about love in the place of *vengeance:*

> You have heard that it was said, "You shall love your neighbor and hate your enemy." But I say to you, Love your enemies and pray for those who persecute you, so that you may be sons of your Father who is in heaven; for he makes his sun rise on the evil and on the good, and he sends rain on the just and the unjust. . . . You, therefore, must be perfect, as your heavenly Father is perfect (Matt. 5:43-45,48).

> Bless those who persecute you; bless and do not curse them. . . . Beloved, never avenge yourselves, but leave it to the wrath of God, for it is written, "Vengeance is mine, I will repay, says the Lord." . . . Do not be overcome by evil, but overcome evil with good (Rom. 12:14,19).

This is the most extreme claim made in this regard. But notice, these *ethical statements* are in fact *theological claims.* What we are to *do* relates to *who God is:* "Be perfect, as your heavenly Father is perfect." The possiblity of a vengeance-free ethic is rooted in the staggering reality of God. And so we are driven to the crucifixion, in which God has decisively dealt with the reality of evil which must be judged. God has responded with "his" own powerful inclination for justice. There is no less of vengeance in the New Testament. But God has wrought it in "his" own person, and so the world has been purged and grace has overcome.

For those who are troubled about the Psalms of vengeance, there is a way beyond them. But it is not an easy or "natural way." It is not the way of careless religious goodwill. It is not the way of moral indifference or flippancy. It is, rather, the way of crucifixion, of accepting the rage and grief and terror of evil in ourselves in order to be liberated for compassion toward others. In the gospel, Christians know "a more excellent way" (1 Cor. 12:31). But it is not the first way. My hunch is that there is a way *beyond* the Psalms of vengeance, but it is a way *through* them and not *around* them. And that is so because of what in fact goes on with us. Willy-nilly, we are vengeful creatures. Thus these harsh Psalms must be fully embraced as our own. Our rage and indignation must be fully *owned* and fully *expressed*. And then (only then) can our rage and indignation be *yielded* to the mercy of God. In taking this route through them, we take the route God "himself" has gone. We are not permitted a cheaper, easier, more "enlightened" way.[6]

Notes

1. Stated in his Preface to the *Commentary on Psalms*. See Ford Lewis Battles, *The Piety of John Calvin* (Grand Rapids: Baker Book House, 1978), p. 27.

2. Terrien, *The Elusive Presence*, p. 316, observes the function and power of "Thou" in Ps. 73: "An inquisitive essay has become a prayer. The skeptic, who pondered intellectual answers to difficult questions, suddenly addressed the Deity as 'Thou.' He inserted his doubt into the context of his adoration. . . . Therefore, he no longer pursued his trend of thinking

within the confines of his autonomous self but pursued it instead in the presence of the Godhead."

3. Masculine pronouns are placed in quotes to indicate the problem of using masculine language when in fact the language is inclusive. I have appropriated the practice from Norman Gottwald, *The Tribes of Yahweh* (Maryknoll, NY: Orbis Books, 1979), pp. 684-685.

4. On the theme of "reversal of fortune," see ibid., pp. 534-540. His focus is on the Song of Hannah. And that in turn is reflected in the Magnificat of Mary. Gottwald is especially attentive to the way in which reversal, which is a literary-rhetorical event, may be evocative of a political-economic reversal.

5. George Mendenhall, *The Tenth Generation* (Baltimore: Johns Hopkins University Press, 1973), chap. 3, has provided an especially helpful discussion of vengeance. It is his argument that vengeance is a political idea and ought not to be understood as a raw, primitive seeking of retaliation. Rather, it is the maintenance of political order and sovereignty in an established "Imperium." The responsible Lord intervenes to right situations which have departed from the over-all governing pattern. Thus vengeance is both punishment and vindication in Israel. While I have not followed Mendenhall precisely, his essay is especially suggestive.

6. Marie Augusta Neal, *A Socio-Theology of Letting Go* (New York: Paulist Press, 1975), discusses the need for "relinquishment" of an economic kind. To be viable such economic relinquishment must be matched by linguistic, liturgical, emotional "letting go."

Psalms

BOOK I

1 Blessed is the man
who walks not in the counsel of
the wicked,
nor stands in the way of sinners,
nor sits in the seat of scoffers;
2 but his delight is in the law of the
LORD,
and on his law he meditates day
and night.
3 He is like a tree
planted by streams of water,
that yields its fruit in its season,
and its leaf does not wither.
In all that he does, he prospers.

4 The wicked are not so,
but are like chaff which the wind
drives away.
5 Therefore the wicked will not stand
in the judgment,
nor sinners in the congregation of
the righteous;
6 for the LORD knows the way of the
righteous,
but the way of the wicked will
perish.

2 Why do the nations conspire,
and the peoples plot in vain?
2 The kings of the earth set themselves,
and the rulers take counsel together,
against the LORD and his
anointed, saying,
3 "Let us burst their bonds asunder,
and cast their cords from us."

4 He who sits in the heavens laughs;
the LORD has them in derision.

5 Then he will speak to them in his
wrath,
and terrify them in his fury, saying,
6 "I have set my king
on Zion, my holy hill."

7 I will tell of the decree of the LORD:
He said to me, "You are my son,
today I have begotten you.
8 Ask of me, and I will make the nations your heritage,
and the ends of the earth your
possession.
9 You shall break them with a rod of
iron,
and dash them in pieces like a
potter's vessel."

10 Now therefore, O kings, be wise;
be warned, O rulers of the earth.
11 Serve the LORD with fear,
with trembling 12 kiss his feet,
lest he be angry, and you perish in
the way;
for his wrath is quickly kindled.
Blessed are all who take refuge in
him.

A Psalm of David, when he fled from
Absalom his son.

3 O LORD, how many are my foes!
Many are rising against me;
2 many are saying of me,
there is no help for him in God.
Selah

3 But thou, O LORD, art a shield about
me,
my glory, and the lifter of my
head.

⁴I cry aloud to the LORD,
   and he answers me from his holy
     hill. *Selah*
⁵I lie down and sleep;
   I wake again, for the LORD sus-
     tains me.
⁶I am not afraid of ten thousands of
     people
   who have set themselves against
     me round about.

⁷Arise, O LORD!
   Deliver me, O my God!
  For thou dost smite all my enemies
     on the cheek,
     thou dost break the teeth of the
     wicked.
⁸Deliverance belongs to the LORD;
   thy blessing be upon thy people!
                Selah

To the choirmaster: with stringed instruments. A Psalm of David.

4 Answer me when I call, O God
     of my right!
  Thou hast given me room when I
     was in distress.
  Be gracious to me, and hear my
     prayer.

²O men, how long shall my honor
     suffer shame?
   How long will you love vain
     words, and seek after lies? *Selah*
³But know that the LORD has set
     apart the godly for himself;
  the LORD hears when I call to him.

⁴Be angry, but sin not;
   commune with your own hearts
     on your beds, and be si-
     lent. *Selah*
⁵Offer right sacrifices,
   and put your trust in the LORD.

⁶There are many who say, "O that we
     might see some good!
  Lift up the light of thy counte-
     nance upon us, O LORD!"
⁷Thou hast put more joy in my heart
   than they have when their grain
     and wine abound.

⁸In peace I will both lie down and
     sleep;

for thou alone, O LORD, makest
   me dwell in safety.

To the choirmaster: for the flutes.
   A Psalm of David.

5 Give ear to my words, O LORD;
    give heed to my groaning.
²Hearken to the wound of my cry,
   my King and my God,
   for to thee do I pray.
³O LORD, in the morning thou dost
     hear my voice;
  in the morning I prepare a sac-
     rifice for thee, and watch.

⁴For thou art not a God who delights
     in wickedness;
  evil may not sojourn with thee.
⁵The boastful may not stand before
     thy eyes;
  thou hatest all evildoers.
⁶Thou destroyest those who speak
     lies;
  the LORD abhors bloodthirsty and
     deceitful men.

⁷But I through the abundance of thy
     steadfast love
  will enter thy house,
  I will worship toward thy holy tem-
     ple in the fear of thee.
⁸Lead me, O LORD, in thy righteous-
     ness
   because of my enemies;
  make thy way straight before me.

⁹For there is no truth in their mouth;
   their heart is destruction,
  their throat is an open sepulchre,
   they flatter with their tongue.
¹⁰Make them bear their guilt, O God;
   let them fall by their own coun-
     sels;
  because of their many transgres-
     sions cast them out,
   for they have rebelled against
     thee.

¹¹But let all who take refuge in thee
     rejoice,
   let them ever sing for joy;
  and do thou defend them,
   that those who love thy name may
     exult in thee.

12 For thou dost bless the righteous, O
LORD;
thou dost cover him with favor as
with a shield.

To the choirmaster: with stringed
instruments; according to
The Sheminith.
A Psalm of David.

6 O LORD, rebuke me not in thy
anger,
nor chasten me in thy wrath.
2 Be gracious to me, O LORD, for I am
languishing;
O LORD, heal me, for my bones
are troubled.
3 My soul also is sorely troubled.
But thou, O LORD—how long?

4 Turn, O LORD, save my life;
deliver me for the sake of thy
steadfast love.
5 For in death there is no remembrance of thee;
in Sheol who can give thee praise?

6 I am weary with my moaning;
every night I flood my bed with
tears;
I drench my couch with my weeping.
7 My eye wastes away because of
grief,
it grows weak because of all my
foes.

8 Depart from me, all you workers of
evil;
for the LORD has heard the sound
of my weeping.
9 The LORD has heard my supplication;
the LORD accepts my prayer.
10 All my enemies shall be ashamed
and sorely troubled;
they shall turn back, and be put to
shame in a moment.

A Shiggaion of David, which he sang
to the LORD concerning Cush a
Benjaminite.

7 O LORD my God, in thee do I take
refuge;

save me from all my pursuers, and
deliver me,
2 lest like a lion they rend me,
dragging me away, with none to
rescue.

3 O LORD my God, if I have done this,
if there is wrong in my hands,
4 if I have requited my friend with
evil
or plundered my enemy without
cause,
5 let the enemy pursue me and over-
take me,
and let him trample my life to the
ground,
and lay my soul in the dust. Selah

6 Arise, O LORD, in thy anger,
lift thyself up against the fury of
my enemies;
awake, O my God; thou hast appointed a judgment.
7 Let the assembly of the peoples be
gathered about thee;
and over it take thy seat on high.
8 The LORD judges the peoples;
judge me, O LORD, according to
my righteousness
and according to the integrity that
is in me.

9 O let the evil of the wicked come to
an end,
but establish thou the righteous,
thou who triest the minds and
hearts,
thou righteous God.
10 My shield is with God,
who saves the upright in heart.
11 God is a righteous judge,
and a God who has indignation
every day.

12 If a man does not repent, God will
whet his sword;
he has bent and strung his bow;
13 he has prepared his deadly weapons,
making his arrows fiery shafts.

14 Behold, the wicked man conceives
evil,
and is pregnant with mischief,
and brings forth lies.
15 He makes a pit, digging it out,
and falls into the hole which he
has made.

16His mischief returns upon his own
head,
and on his own pate his violence
descends.
17I will give to the LORD the thanks
due to his righteousness,
and I will sing praise to the name
of the LORD, the Most High.

To the choirmaster: according to The
Gittith. A Psalm of David.

8 O LORD, our Lord,
how majestic is thy name in all
the earth!
Thou whose glory above the heavens is chanted
2 by the mouth of babes and infants,
thou hast founded a bulwark because of thy foes,
to still the enemy and the avenger.

3When I look at thy heavens, the
work of thy fingers,
the moon and the stars which
thou hast established;
4what is man that thou art mindful of
him,
and the son of man that thou dost
care for him?

5Yet thou hast made him little less
than God,
and dost crown him with glory
and honor.
6Thou hast given him dominion over
the works of thy hands;
thou hast put all things under his
feet,
7all sheep and oxen,
and also the beasts of the field,
8the birds of the air, and the fish of
the sea,
whatever passes along the paths
of the sea.
9O LORD, our Lord,
how majestic is thy name in all the
earth!

To the choirmaster: according to
Muth-labben. A Psalm of David.

9 I will give thanks to the LORD
with my whole heart;

I will tell of all thy wonderful
deeds.
2I will be glad and exult in thee,
I will sing praise to thy name, O
Most High.

3When my enemies turned back,
they stumbled and perished before thee.
4For thou hast maintained my just
cause;
thou hast sat on the throne giving
righteous judgment.
5Thou hast rebuked the nations, thou
hast destroyed the wicked;
thou hast blotted out their name
for ever and ever.
6The enemy have vanished in everlasting ruins;
their cities thou hast rooted out;
the very memory of them has
perished.

7But the LORD sits enthroned for
ever,
he has established his throne for
judgment;
8and he judges the world with righteousness,
he judges the peoples with equity.

9The LORD is a stronghold for the
oppressed,
a stronghold in times of trouble.
10And those who know thy name put
their trust in thee,
for thou, O LORD, hast not forsak-
en those who seek thee.

11Sing praises to the LORD, who
dwells in Zion!
Tell among the peoples his deeds!
12For he who avenges blood is mindful of them;
he does not forget the cry of the
afflicted.

13Be gracious to me, O LORD!
Behold what I suffer from those
who hate me,
O thou who liftest me up from the
gates of death,
14that I may recount all thy praises,
that in the gates of the daughter of
Zion
I may rejoice in thy deliverance.

15 The nations have sunk in the pit
which they made;
in the net which they hid has their
own foot been caught.
16 The LORD has made himself known,
he has executed judgment;
the wicked are snared in the work
of their own hands.
Higgaion. Selah

17 The wicked shall depart to Sheol,
all the nations that forget God.
18 For the needy shall not always be
forgotten,
and the hope of the poor shall not
perish for ever.

19 Arise, O LORD! Let not man prevail;
let the nations be judged before
thee!
20 Put them in fear, O LORD!
Let the nations know that they are
but men! *Selah*

10 Why dost thou stand afar off,
O LORD?
Why dost thou hide thyself in times
of trouble?
2 In arrogance the wicked hotly pursue the poor;
let them be caught in the schemes
which they have devised.

3 For the wicked boasts of the desires
of his heart,
and the man greedy for gain
curses and renounces the LORD.
4 In the pride of his countenance the
wicked does not seek him;
all his thoughts are, "There is no
God."

5 His ways prosper at all times;
thy judgments are on high, out of
his sight;
as for all his foes, he puffs at
them.
6 He thinks in his heart, "I shall not
be moved;
throughout all generations I shall
not meet adversity."

7 His mouth is filled with cursing and
deceit and oppression;
under his tongue are mischief and
iniquity.

8 He sits in ambush in the villages;
in hiding places he murders the
innocent.

His eyes stealthily watch for the
hapless,
9 he lurks in secret like a lion in his
covert;
he lurks that he may seize the poor,
he seizes the poor when he draws
him into his net.

10 The hapless is crushed, sinks down,
and falls by his might.
11 He thinks in his heart, "God has
forgotten,
he has hidden his face, he will
never see it."

12 Arise, O LORD; O God, lift up thy
hand;
forget not the afflicted.
13 Why does the wicked renounce
God,
and say in his heart, "Thou wilt
not call to account"?

14 Thou dost see; yea, thou dost note
trouble and vexation,
that thou mayst take it into thy
hands;
the hapless commits himself to thee;
thou hast been the helper of the
fatherless.

15 Break thou the arm of the wicked
and evildoer;
seek out his wickedness till thou
find none.
16 The LORD is king for ever and ever;
the nations shall perish from his
land.

17 O LORD, thou wilt hear the desire of
the meek;
thou wilt strengthen their heart,
thou wilt incline thy ear
18 to do justice to the fatherless and the
oppressed,
so that man who is of the earth
may strike terror no more.

To the choirmaster. Of David.

11 In the LORD I take refuge;
how can you say to me,

"Flee like a bird to the mountains;
² for lo, the wicked bend the bow,
they have fitted their arrow to the
string,
to shoot in the dark at the upright
in heart;
³ if the foundations are destroyed,
what can the righteous do?"

⁴ The LORD is in his holy temple,
the LORD's throne is in heaven;
his eyes behold, his eyelids test,
the children of men.
⁵ The LORD tests the righteous and
the wicked,
and his soul hates him that loves
violence.
⁶ On the wicked he will rain coals of
fire and brimstone;
a scorching wind shall be the portion of their cup.
⁷ For the LORD is righteous, he loves
righteous deeds;
the upright shall behold his face.

To the choirmaster: according to
The Sheminith. A Psalm of David.

12 Help, LORD; for there is no
longer any that is godly;
for the faithful have vanished
from among the sons of men.
² Every one utters lies to his neighbor;
with flattering lips and a double
heart they speak.

³ May the LORD cut off all flattering
lips,
the tongue that makes great
boasts,
⁴ those who say, "With our tongue we
will prevail,
our lips are with us; who is our
master?"

⁵ "Because the poor are despoiled, because the needy groan,
I will now arise," says the LORD;
"I will place him in the safety for
which he longs."
⁶ The promises of the LORD are promises that are pure,
silver refined in a furnace on the
ground,
purified seven times.

⁷ Do thou, O LORD, protect us,
guard us ever from this generation.
⁸ On every side the wicked prowl,
as vileness is exalted among the
sons of men.

To the choirmaster. A Psalm of David.

13 How long, O LORD? Wilt thou
forget me for ever?
How long wilt thou hide thy face
from me?
² How long must I bear pain in my
soul,
and have sorrow in my heart all
the day?
How long shall my enemy be exalted
over me?

³ Consider and answer me, O LORD
my God;
lighten my eyes, lest I sleep the
sleep of death;
⁴ lest my enemy say, "I have prevailed
over him";
lest my foes rejoice because I am
shaken.

⁵ But I have trusted in thy steadfast
love;
my heart shall rejoice in thy salvation.
⁶ I will sing to the LORD,
because he has dealt bountifully
with me.

To the choirmaster. Of David.

14 The fool says in his heart,
"There is no God."
They are corrupt, they do abominable deeds,
there is none that does good.

² The LORD looks down from heaven
upon the children of men,
to see if there are any that act
wisely,
that seek after God.

³ They have all gone astray, they are
all alike corrupt;
there is none that does good,
no, not one.

⁴ Have they no knowledge, all the
    evildoers
  who eat up my people as they eat
    bread,
  and do not call upon the LORD?

⁵ There they shall be in great terror,
  for God is with the generation of
    the righteous.
⁶ You would confound the plans of the
    poor,
  but the LORD is his refuge.

⁷ O that deliverance for Israel would
    come out of Zion!
  When the LORD restores the for-
    tunes of his people,
  Jacob shall rejoice, Israel shall be
    glad.

A Psalm of David.

15 O LORD, who shall sojourn in
    thy tent?
Who shall dwell on thy holy hill?

² He who walks blamelessly, and does
    what is right,
  and speaks truth from his heart;
³ who does not slander with his
    tongue,
  and does no evil to his friend,
  nor takes up a reproach against
    his neighbor;
⁴ in whose eyes a reprobate is de-
    spised,
  but who honors those who fear
    the LORD;
  who swears to his own hurt and
    does not change;
⁵ who does not put out his money at
    interest,
  and does not take a bribe against
    the innocent.

He who does these things shall
  never be moved.

A Miktam of David.

16 Preserve me, O God, for in thee
    I take refuge.
  ²I say to the LORD, "Thou art my
    Lord;
  I have no good apart from thee."

³ As for the saints in the land, they are
    the noble,
  in whom is all my delight.

⁴ Those who choose another god mul-
    tiply their sorrows;
  their libations of blood I will not
    pour out
  or take their names upon my lips.

⁵ The LORD is my chosen portion and
    my cup;
  thou holdest my lot.
⁶ The lines have fallen for me in
    pleasant places;
  yea, I have a goodly heritage.

⁷ I bless the LORD who gives me
    counsel;
  in the night also my heart in-
    structs me.
⁸ I keep the LORD always before me;
  because he is at my right hand, I
    shall not be moved.

⁹ Therefore my heart is glad, and my
    soul rejoices;
  my body also dwells secure.
¹⁰ For thou dost not give me up to
    Sheol,
  or let thy godly one see the Pit.

¹¹ Thou dost show me the path of life;
  in thy presence there is fulness of
    joy,
  in thy right hand are pleasures for
    evermore.

A Prayer of David.

17 Hear a just cause, O LORD;
    attend to my cry!
Give ear to my prayer from lips free
  of deceit!
² From thee let my vindication come!
  Let thy eyes see the right!

³ If thou triest my heart, if thou
    visitest me by night,
  if thou testest me, thou wilt find
    no wickedness in me;
  my mouth does not transgress.
⁴ With regard to the works of men,
  by the word of thy lips
  I have avoided the ways of the
    violent.

⁵ My steps have held fast to thy paths,
    my feet have not slipped.

⁶ I call upon thee, for thou wilt answer
    me, O God;
    incline thy ear to me, hear my
    words.
⁷ Wondrously show thy steadfast love,
    O savior of those who seek refuge
    from their adversaries at thy right
    hand.
⁸ Keep me as the apple of the eye;
    hide me in the shadow of thy
    wings,
⁹ from the wicked who despoil me,
    my deadly enemies who surround
    me.
¹⁰ They close their hearts to pity;
    with their mouths they speak ar-
    rogantly.
¹¹ They track me down; now they sur-
    round me;
    they set their eyes to cast me to
    the ground.
¹² They are like a lion eager to tear,
    as a young lion lurking in am-
    bush.

¹³ Arise, O LORD! confront them, over-
    throw them!
    Deliver my life from the wicked
    by thy sword,
¹⁴ from men by thy hand, O LORD,
    from men whose portion in life is
    of the world.
    May their belly be filled with what
    thou hast stored up for them;
    may their children have more than
    enough;
    may they leave something over to
    their babes.
¹⁵ As for me, I shall behold thy face in
    righteousness;
    when I awake, I shall be satisfied
    with beholding thy form.

To the choirmaster. A Psalm of David
the servant of the LORD, who addressed the words of this song to the
LORD on the day when the LORD delivered him from the hand of all his
enemies, and from the hand of Saul.
He said:

18   I love thee, O LORD, my
    strength.

² The LORD is my rock, and my for-
    tress, and my deliverer,
    my God, my rock, in whom I take
    refuge,
    my shield, and the horn of my
    salvation, my stronghold.
³ I call upon the LORD, who is worthy
    to be praised,
    and I am saved from my enemies.

⁴ The cords of death encompassed
    me,
    the torrents of perdition assailed
    me;
⁵ the cords of Sheol entangled me,
    the snares of death confronted me.
⁶ In my distress I called upon the
    LORD;
    to my God I cried for help.
    From his temple he heard my voice,
    and my cry to him reached his
    ears.

⁷ Then the earth reeled and rocked;
    the foundations also of the
    mountains trembled
    and quaked, because he was an-
    gry.
⁸ Smoke went up from his nostrils,
    and devouring fire from his
    mouth;
    glowing coals flamed forth from
    him.
⁹ He bowed the heavens, and came
    down;
    thick darkness was under his feet.
¹⁰ He rode on a cherub, and flew;
    he came swiftly upon the wings of
    the wind.
¹¹ He made darkness his covering
    around him,
    his canopy thick clouds dark with
    water.
¹² Out of the brightness before him
    there broke through his clouds
    hailstones and coals of fire.
¹³ The LORD also thundered in the
    heavens,
    and the Most High uttered his
    voice,
    hailstones and coals of fire.
¹⁴ And he sent out his arrows, and
    scattered them;
    he flashed forth lightnings, and
    routed them.
¹⁵ Then the channels of the sea were
    seen,

and the foundations of the world
were laid bare,
at thy rebuke, O LORD,
at the blast of the breath of thy
nostrils.

16 He reached from on high, he took
me,
he drew me out of many waters.

17 He delivered me from my strong
enemy,
and from those who hated me;
for they were too mighty for me.

18 They came upon me in the day of
my calamity;
but the LORD was my stay.

19 He brought me forth into a broad
place;
he delivered me, because he delighted in me.

20 The LORD rewarded me according to
my righteousness;
according to the cleanness of my
hands he recompensed me.

21 For I have kept the ways of the
LORD,
and have not wickedly departed
from my God.

22 For all his ordinances were before
me,
and his statutes I did not put away
from me.

23 I was blameless before him,
and I kept myself from guilt.

24 Therefore the LORD has recompensed me according to my
righteousness,
according to the cleanness of my
hands in his sight.

25 With the loyal thou dost show thyself loyal;
with the blameless man thou dost
show thyself blameless;

26 with the pure thou dost show thyself pure;
and with the crooked thou dost
show thyself perverse.

27 For thou dost deliver a humble
people;
but the haughty eyes thou dost
bring down.

28 Yea, thou dost light my lamp;
the LORD my God lightens my
darkness.

29 Yea, by thee I can crush a troop;
and by my God I can leap over a
wall.

30 This God—his way is perfect;
the promise of the LORD proves
true;
he is a shield for all those who
take refuge in him.

31 For who is God, but the LORD?
And who is a rock, except our
God?—

32 the God who girded me with
strength,
and made my way safe.

33 He made my feet like hinds' feet,
and set me secure on the
heights.

34 He trains my hands for war,
so that my arms can bend a bow of
bronze.

35 Thou hast given me the shield of thy
salvation,
and thy right hand supported me,
and thy help made me great.

36 Thou didst give a wide place for my
steps under me,
and my feet did not slip.

37 I pursued my enemies and overtook
them;
and did not turn back till they
were consumed.

38 I thrust them through, so that they
were not able to rise;
they fell under my feet.

39 For thou didst gird me with strength
for the battle;
thou didst make my assailants
sink under me.

40 Thou didst make my enemies turn
their backs to me,
and those who hated me I destroyed.

41 They cried for help, but there was
none to save,
they cried to the LORD, but he did
not answer them.

42 I beat them fine as dust before the
wind;
I cast them out like the mire of the
streets.

43 Thou didst deliver me from strife
with the peoples;
thou didst make me the head of
the nations;
people whom I had not known
served me.

44 As soon as they heard of me they
obeyed me;

foreigners came cringing to me.
45 Foreigners lost heart,
and came trembling out of their
fastnesses.

46 The LORD lives; and blessed be my
rock,
and exalted be the God of my salvation,
47 the God who gave me vengeance
and subdued peoples under me;
48 who delivered me from my enemies;
yea, thou didst exalt me above my
adversaries;
thou didst deliver me from men of
violence.

49 For this I will extol thee, O LORD,
among the nations,
and sing praises to thy name.
50 Great triumphs he gives to his king,
and shows steadfast love to his
anointed,
to David and his descendants for
ever.

To the choirmaster. A Psalm of David.

19 The heavens are telling the
glory of God;
and the firmament proclaims his
handiwork.
2 Day to day pours forth speech,
and night to night declares
knowledge.
3 There is no speech, nor are there
words;
their voice is not heard;
4 yet their voice goes out through all
the earth,
and their words to the end of the
world.

In them he has set a tent for the sun,
5 which comes forth like a bride-
groom leaving his chamber,
and like a strong man runs its
course with joy.
6 Its rising is from the end of the
heavens,
and its circuit to the end of them;
and there is nothing hid from its
heat.

7 The law of the LORD is perfect,
reviving the soul;

the testimony of the LORD is sure,
making wise the simple;
8 the precepts of the LORD are right,
rejoicing the heart;
the commandment of the LORD is
pure,
enlightening the eyes;
9 the fear of the LORD is clean,
enduring for ever;
the ordinances of the LORD are true,
and righteous altogether.
10 More to be desired are they than
gold,
even much fine gold;
sweeter also than honey
and drippings of the honeycomb.

11 Moreover by them is thy servant
warned;
in keeping them there is great reward.
12 But who can discern his errors?
Clear thou me from hidden faults.
13 Keep back thy servant also from presumptuous sins;
let them not have dominion over
me!
Then I shall be blameless,
and innocent of great transgression.

14 Let the words of my mouth and the
meditation of my heart
be acceptable in thy sight,
O LORD, my rock and my redeemer.

To the choirmaster. A Psalm of David.

20 The LORD answer you in the
day of trouble!
The name of the God of Jacob protect you!
2 May he send you help from the sanctuary,
and give you support from Zion!
3 May he remember all your offerings,
and regard with favor your burnt
sacrifices!   Selah
4 May he grant you your heart's desire,
and fulfil all your plans!
5 May we shout for joy over your
victory,
and in the name of our God set up
our banners!

May the LORD fulfil all your petitions!

6 Now I know that the LORD will help
his anointed;
he will answer him from his holy
heaven
with mighty victories by his right
hand.
7 Some boast of chariots, and some of
horses;
but we boast of the name of the
LORD our God.
8 They will collapse and fall;
but we shall rise and stand upright.

9 Give victory to the king, O LORD;
answer us when we call.

To the choirmaster. A Psalm of David.

21 In thy strength the king rejoices, O LORD;
and in thy help how greatly he
exults!
2 Thou hast given him his heart's desire,
and hast not withheld the request
of his lips.   Selah
3 For thou dost meet him with goodly
blessings;
thou dost set a crown of fine gold
upon his head.
4 He asked life of thee; thou gavest it
to him,
length of days for ever and ever.
5 His glory is great through thy help;
splendor and majesty thou dost
bestow upon him.
6 Yea, thou dost make him most
blessed for ever;
thou dost make him glad with the
joy of thy presence.
7 For the king trusts in the LORD;
and through the steadfast love of
the Most High he shall not be
moved.

8 Your hand will find out all your
enemies;
your right hand will find out
those who hate you.
9 You will make them as a blazing
oven when you appear.

The LORD will swallow them up in
his wrath;
and fire will consume them.
10 You will destroy their offspring from
the earth,
and their children from among the
sons of men.
11 If they plan evil against you,
if they devise mischief, they will
not succeed.
12 For you will put them to flight;
you will aim at their faces with
your bows.
13 Be exalted, O LORD, in thy strength!
We will sing and praise thy power.

To the choirmaster: according to The
Hind of the Dawn. A Psalm of David.

22 My God, my God, why hast
thou forsaken me?
Why are thou so far from helping
me, from the words of my
groaning?
2 O my God, I cry by day, but thou
dost not answer;
and by night, but find no rest.

3 Yet thou art holy,
enthroned on the praises of Israel.
4 In thee our fathers trusted;
they trusted, and thou didst deliver them.
5 To thee they cried, and were saved;
in thee they trusted, and were not
disappointed.

6 But I am a worm, and no man;
scorned by men, and despised by
the people.
7 All who see me mock at me,
they make mouths at me, they
wag their heads;
8 "He committed his cause to the
LORD; let him deliver him,
let him rescue him, for he delights
in him!"

9 Yet thou art he who took me from
the womb;
thou didst keep me safe upon my
mother's breasts.
10 Upon thee was I cast from my birth,
and since my mother bore me
thou hast been my God.

11 Be not far from me,
for trouble is near
and there is none to help.

12 Many bulls encompass me,
strong bulls of Bashan surround
me;
13 they open wide their mouths at me,
like a ravening and roaring lion.
14 I am poured out like water,
and all my bones are out of joint;
my heart is like wax,
it is melted within my breast;
15 my strength is dried up like a pot-
sherd,
and my tongue cleaves to my
jaws;
thou dost lay me in the dust of
death.

16 Yea, dogs are round about me;
a company of evildoers encircle
me;
they have pierced my hands and
feet—
17 I can count all my bones—
they stare and gloat over me;
18 they divide my garments among
them,
and for my raiment they cast lots.

19 But thou, O LORD, be not far off!
O thou my help, hasten to my aid!
20 Deliver my soul from the sword,
my life from the power of the dog!
21 Save me from the mouth of the lion,
my afflicted soul from the horns of
the wild oxen!

22 I will tell of thy name to my brethren;
in the midst of the congregation I
will praise thee:
23 You who fear the LORD, praise him!
all you sons of Jacob, glorify him,
and stand in awe of him, all you
sons of Israel!
24 For he has not despised or abhorred
the affliction of the afflicted;
and he has not hid his face from
him,
but he has heard, when he cried
to him.
25 From thee comes my praise in the
great congregation;
my vows I will pay before those
who fear him.

26 The afflicted shall eat and be satis-
fied;
those who seek him shall praise
the LORD!
May your hearts live for ever!

27 All the ends of the earth shall remember
and turn to the LORD;
and all the families of the nations
shall worship before him.
28 For dominion belongs to the LORD,
and he rules over the nations.

29 Yea, to him shall all the proud of the
earth bow down;
before him shall bow all who go
down to the dust,
and he who cannot keep himself
alive.
30 Posterity shall serve him;
men shall tell of the Lord to the
coming generation,
31 and proclaim his deliverance to a
people yet unborn,
that he has wrought it.

A Psalm of David.

23 The LORD is my shepherd, I
shall not want;
2 he makes me lie down in green
pastures.
He leads me beside still waters;
3 he restores my soul.
He leads me in paths of righteousness
for his name's sake.

4 Even though I walk through the valley of the shadow of death,
I fear no evil;
for thou art with me;
thy rod and thy staff,
they comfort me.

5 Thou preparest a table before me
in the presence of my enemies;
thou anointest my head with oil,
my cup overflows.
6 Surely goodness and mercy shall follow me
all the days of my life;
and I shall dwell in the house of the
LORD
for ever.

A Psalm of David.

24 The earth is the LORD's and the fulness thereof,
the world and those who dwell therein;
2 for he has founded it upon the seas,
and established it upon the rivers.

3 Who shall ascend the hill of the LORD?
And who shall stand in his holy place?
4 He who has clean hands and a pure heart,
who does not lift up his soul to what is false,
and does not swear deceitfully.
5 He will receive blessing from the LORD,
and vindication from the God of his salvation.
6 Such is the generation of those who seek him,
who seek the face of the God of Jacob.   *Selah*

7 Lift up your heads, O gates!
and be lifted up, O ancient doors!
that the King of glory may come in.
8 Who is the King of glory?
The LORD, strong and mighty,
the LORD, mighty in battle!
9 Lift up your heads, O gates!
and be lifted up, O ancient doors!
that the King of glory may come in.
10 Who is this King of glory?
The LORD of hosts,
he is the King of glory!   *Selah*

A Psalm of David.

25 To thee, O LORD, I lift up my soul.
2 O my God, in thee I trust,
let me not be put to shame;
let not my enemies exult over me.
3 Yea, let none that wait for thee be put to shame;
let them be ashamed who are wantonly treacherous.
4 Make me to know thy ways, O LORD;

teach me thy paths.
5 Lead me in thy truth, and teach me,
for thou art the God of my salvation;
for thee I wait all the day long.

6 Be mindful of thy mercy, O LORD,
and of thy steadfast love,
for they have been from of old.
7 Remember not the sins of my youth,
or my transgressions;
according to thy steadfast love remember me,
for thy goodness' sake, O LORD!

8 Good and upright is the LORD;
therefore he instructs sinners in the way.
9 He leads the humble in what is right,
and teaches the humble his way.
10 All the paths of the LORD are steadfast love and faithfulness,
for those who keep his covenant and his testimonies.

11 For thy name's sake, O LORD,
pardon my guilt, for it is great.
12 Who is the man that fears the LORD?
Him will he instruct in the way that he should choose.
13 He himself shall abide in prosperity,
and his children shall possess the land.
14 The friendship of the LORD is for those who fear him,
and he makes known to them his covenant.
15 My eyes are ever toward the LORD,
for he will pluck my feet out of the net.
16 Turn thou to me, and be gracious to me;
for I am lonely and afflicted.
17 Relieve the troubles of my heart,
and bring me out of my distresses.
18 Consider my affliction and my trouble,
and forgive all my sins.

19 Consider how many are my foes,
and with what violent hatred they hate me.
20 Oh guard my life, and deliver me;
let me not be put to shame, for I take refuge in thee.

21 May integrity and uprightness preserve me,
for I wait for thee.
22 Redeem Israel, O God,
out of all his troubles.

A Psalm of David.

26 Vindicate me, O LORD,
for I have walked in my integrity,
and I have trusted in the LORD
without wavering.
2 Prove me, O LORD, and try me;
test my heart and my mind.
3 For thy steadfast love is before my
eyes,
and I walk in faithfulness to thee.

4 I do not sit with false men,
nor do I consort with dissemblers;
5 I hate the company of evildoers,
and I will not sit with the wicked.

6 I wash my hands in innocence,
and go about thy altar, O LORD,
7 singing aloud a song of thanksgiving,
and telling all thy wondrous
deeds.

8 O LORD, I love the habitation of thy
house,
and the place where thy glory
dwells.
9 Sweep me not away with sinners,
nor my life with bloodthirsty
men,
10 men in whose hands are evil devices,
and whose right hands are full of
bribes.

11 But as for me, I walk in my integrity;
redeem me, and be gracious to
me.
12 My foot stands on level ground;
in the great congregation I will
bless the LORD.

A Psalm of David.

27 The LORD is my light and my
salvation;
whom shall I fear?

The LORD is the stronghold of my
life;
of whom shall I be afraid?

2 When evildoers assail me,
uttering slanders against me,
my adversaries and foes,
they shall stumble and fall.
3 Though a host encamp against me,
my heart shall not fear;
though war arise against me,
yet I will be confident.

4 One thing have I asked of the LORD,
that will I seek after;
that I may dwell in the house of the
LORD
all the days of my life,
to behold the beauty of the LORD,
and to inquire in his temple.

5 For he will hide me in his shelter in
the day of trouble;
he will conceal me under the cover
of his tent,
he will set me high upon a rock.

6 And now my head shall be lifted up
above my enemies round about
me;
and I will offer in his tent
sacrifices with shouts of joy;
I will sing and make melody to the
LORD.

7 Hear, O LORD, when I cry aloud,
be gracious to me and answer me!
8 Thou hast said, "Seek ye my face."
My heart says to thee,
"Thy face, LORD, do I seek."
9   Hide not thy face from me.

Turn not thy servant away in anger,
thou who hast been my help.
Cast me not off, forsake me not,
O God of my salvation!
10 For my father and my mother have
forsaken me,
but the LORD will take me up.
11 Teach me thy way, O LORD;
and lead me on a level path
because of my enemies.
12 Give me not up to the will of my
adversaries;
for false witnesses have risen
against me,
and they breathe out violence.

¹³I believe that I shall see the goodness of the LORD
in the land of the living!
¹⁴Wait for the LORD;
be strong, and let your heart take
courage;
yea, wait for the LORD!

A Psalm of David.

28 To thee, O LORD, I call;
my rock, be not deaf to me,
lest, if thou be silent to me,
I become like those who go down
to the Pit.
²Hear the voice of my supplication,
as I cry to thee for help,
as I lift up my hands
toward thy most holy sanctuary.

³Take me not off with the wicked,
with those who are workers of
evil,
who speak peace with their
neighbors,
while mischief is in their hearts.
⁴Requite them according to their
work,
and according to the evil of their
deeds;
requite them according to the work
of their hands;
render them their due reward.
⁵Because they do not regard the
works of the LORD,
or the work of his hands,
he will break them down and build
them up no more.

⁶Blessed be the LORD!
for he has heard the voice of my
supplications.
⁷The LORD is my strength and my
shield;
in him my heart trusts;
so I am helped, and my heart exults,
and with my song I give thanks to
him.
⁸The LORD is the strength of his
people,
he is the saving refuge of his
anointed.
⁹O save thy people, and bless thy
heritage;
be thou their shepherd, and carry
them for ever.

A Psalm of David.

29 Ascribe to the LORD, O
heavenly beings,
ascribe to the LORD glory and
strength.
²Ascribe to the LORD the glory of his
name;
worship the LORD in holy array.

³The voice of the LORD is upon the
waters;
the God of glory thunders,
the LORD, upon many waters.
⁴The voice of the LORD is powerful,
the voice of the LORD is full of
majesty.

⁵The voice of the LORD breaks the
cedars,
the LORD breaks the cedars of
Lebanon.
⁶He makes Lebanon to skip like a
calf,
and Sirion like a young wild ox.

⁷The voice of the LORD flashes forth
flames of fire.
⁸The voice of the LORD shakes the
wilderness,
the LORD shakes the wilderness of
Kadesh.
⁹The voice of the LORD makes the
oaks to whirl,
and strips the forests bare;
and in his temple all cry, "Glory!"

¹⁰The LORD sits enthroned over the
flood;
the LORD sits enthroned as king
for ever.
¹¹May the LORD give strength to his
people!
May the LORD bless his people
with peace!

A Psalm of David. A Song at the dedication of the Temple.

30 I will extol thee, O LORD, for
thou has drawn me up,
and hast not let my foes rejoice
over me.
²O LORD my God, I cried to thee for
help,
and thou hast healed me.

3 O Lord, thou hast brought up my
soul from Sheol,
restored me to life from among
those gone down to the Pit.

4 Sing praises to the Lord, O you his
saints,
and give thanks to his holy name.
5 For his anger is but for a moment,
and his favor is for a lifetime.
Weeping may tarry for the night,
but joy comes with the morning.

6 As for me, I said in my prosperity,
"I shall never be moved."
7 By thy favor, O Lord,
thou hadst established me as a
strong mountain;
thou didst hide thy face,
I was dismayed.

8 To thee, O Lord, I cried;
and to the Lord I made supplication:
9 "What profit is there in my death,
if I go down to the Pit?
Will the dust praise thee?
Will it tell of thy faithfulness?
10 Hear, O Lord, and be gracious to
me!
O Lord, be thou my helper!"

11 Thou hast turned for me my mourning into dancing;
thou hast loosed my sackcloth
and girded me with gladness,
12 that my soul may praise thee and
not be silent.
O Lord my God, I will give
thanks to thee for ever.

To the choirmaster. A Psalm of David.

31 In thee, O Lord, do I seek refuge;
let me never be put to shame;
in thy righteousness deliver me!
2 Incline thy ear to me,
rescue me speedily!
Be thou a rock of refuge for me,
a strong fortress to save me!

3 Yea, thou art my rock and my fortress;
for thy name's sake lead me and
guide me,

4 take me out of the net which is hidden for me,
for thou art my refuge.
5 Into thy hand I commit my spirit;
thou hast redeemed me, O Lord,
faithful God.
6 Thou hatest those who pay regard to
vain idols;
but I trust in the Lord.
7 I will rejoice and be glad for thy
steadfast love,
because thou hast seen my affliction,
thou hast taken heed of my adver-
sities,
8 and hast not delivered me into the
hand of the enemy;
thou hast set my feet in a broad
place.

9 Be gracious to me, O Lord, for I am
in distress;
my eye is wasted from grief,
my soul and my body also.
10 For my life is spent with sorrow,
and my years with sighing;
my strength fails because of my
misery,
and my bones waste away.
11 I am the scorn of all my adversaries,
a horror to my neighbors,
an object of dread to my acquain-
tances;
those who see me in the street flee
from me.
12 I have passed out of mind like one
who is dead;
I have become like a broken vessel.
13 Yea, I hear the whispering of
many—terror on every side!—
as they scheme together against me,
as they plot to take my life.

14 But I trust in thee, O Lord,
I say, "Thou art my God."
15 My times are in thy hand;
deliver me from the hand of my
enemies and persecutors!
16 Let thy face shine on thy servant;
save me in thy steadfast love!
17 Let me not be put to shame, O
Lord,
for I call on thee;
let the wicked be put to shame,
let them go dumbfounded to
Sheol.

18 Let the lying lips be dumb,
which speak insolently against
the righteous
in pride and contempt.

19 O how abundant is thy goodness,
which thou hast laid up for those
who fear thee,
and wrought for those who take refuge in thee,
in the sight of the sons of men!
20 In the covert of thy presence thou
hidest them
from the plots of men;
thou holdest them safe under thy
shelter
from the strife of tongues.
21 Blessed be the LORD,
for he has wondrously shown his
steadfast love to me
when I was beset as in a besieged
city.
22 I had said in my alarm,
"I am driven far from thy sight."
But thou didst hear my supplications,
when I cried to thee for help.
23 Love the LORD, all you his saints!
The LORD preserves the faithful,
but abundantly requites him who
acts haughtily.
24 Be strong, and let your heart take
courage,
all you who wait for the LORD!

A Psalm of David. A Maskil.

32 Blessed is he whose transgression is forgiven,
whose sin is covered.
2 Blessed is the man to whom the
LORD imputes no iniquity,
and in whose spirit there is no
deceit.

3 When I declared not my sin, my
body wasted away
through my groaning all day long.
4 For day and night thy hand was
heavy upon me;
my strength was dried up as by
the heat of summer.   Selah
5 I acknowledged my sin to thee,
and I did not hide my iniquity;
I said, "I will confess my transgressions to the LORD";

then thou didst forgive the guilt of
my sin.   Selah
6 Therefore let every one who is godly
offer prayer to thee;
at a time of distress, in the rush of
great waters,
they shall not reach him.
7 Thou art a hiding place for me,
thou preservest me from trouble;
thou dost encompass me with deliverance.   Selah

8 I will instruct you and teach you
the way you should go;
I will counsel you with my eye
upon you.
9 Be not like a horse or a mule, without understanding,
which must be curbed with bit
and bridle,
else it will not keep with you.
10 Many are the pangs of the wicked;
but steadfast love surrounds him
who trusts in the LORD.
11 Be glad in the LORD, and rejoice, O
righteous,
and shout for joy, all you upright
in heart!

33 Rejoice in the LORD, O you
righteous!
Praise befits the upright.
2 Praise the LORD with the lyre,
make melody to him with the
harp of ten strings!
3 Sing to him a new song,
play skilfully on the strings, with
loud shouts.
4 For the word of the LORD is upright;
and all his work is done in faithfulness.
5 He loves righteousness and justice;
the earth is full of the steadfast
love of the LORD.

6 By the word of the LORD the heavens were made,
and all their host by the breath of
his mouth.
7 He gathered the waters of the sea as
in a bottle;
he put the deeps in storehouses.

8 Let all the earth fear the LORD,
let all the inhabitants of the world
stand in awe of him!

9 For he spoke, and it came to be;
he commanded, and it stood
forth.
10 The LORD brings the counsel of the
nations to nought;
he frustrates the plans of the
peoples.
11 The counsel of the LORD stands for
ever,
the thoughts of his heart to all
generations.
12 Blessed is the nation whose God is
the LORD,
the people whom he has chosen as
his heritage!

13 The LORD looks down from heaven,
he sees all the sons of men;
14 from where he sits enthroned he
looks forth
on all the inhabitants of the earth,
15 he who fashions the hearts of them
all,
and observes all their deeds.
16 A king is not saved by his great
army;
a warrior is not delivered by his
great strength.
17 The war horse is a vain hope for
victory,
and by its great might it cannot
save.

18 Behold, the eye of the LORD is on
those who fear him,
on those who hope in his steadfast love,
19 that he may deliver their soul from
death,
and keep them alive in famine.

20 Our soul waits for the LORD;
he is our help and shield.
21 Yea, our heart is glad in him,
because we trust in his holy
name.
22 Let thy steadfast love, O LORD, be
upon us,
even as we hope in thee.

A Psalm of David, when he feigned
madness before Abimelech, so that he
drove him out, and he went away.

34 I will bless the LORD at all
times;

his praise shall continually be in
my mouth.
2 My soul makes its boast in the
LORD;
let the afflicted hear and be glad.
3 O magnify the LORD with me,
and let us exalt his name together!

4 I sought the LORD, and he answered
me,
and delivered me from all my
fears.
5 Look to him, and be radiant;
so your faces shall never be
ashamed.
6 This poor man cried, and the LORD
heard him,
and saved him out of all his troubles.
7 The angel of the LORD encamps
around those who fear him, and
delivers them.
8 O taste and see that the LORD is
good!
Happy is the man who takes refuge in him!
9 O fear the LORD, you his saints,
for those who fear him have no
want!
10 The young lions suffer want and
hunger;
but those who seek the LORD lack
no good thing.

11 Come, O sons, listen to me,
I will teach you the fear of the
LORD.
12 What man is there who desires life,
and covets many days, that he
may enjoy good?
13 Keep your tongue from evil,
and your lips from speaking deceit.
14 Depart from evil, and do good;
seek peace, and pursue it.

15 The eyes of the LORD are toward the
righteous,
and his ears toward their cry.
16 The face of the LORD is against evildoers,
to cut off the remembrance of
them from the earth.
17 When the righteous cry for help,
the LORD hears,
and delivers them out of all their
troubles.

18 The LORD is near to the brokenhearted,
   and saves the crushed in spirit.

19 Many are the afflictions of the righteous;
   but the LORD delivers him out of
   them all.
20 He keeps all his bones;
   not one of them is broken.
21 Evil shall slay the wicked;
   and those who hate the righteous
   will be condemned.
22 The LORD redeems the life of his
   servants;
   none of those who take refuge in
   him will be condemned.

A Psalm of David.

35 Contend, O LORD, with those
who contend with me;
   fight against those who fight
   against me!
2 Take hold of shield and buckler,
   and rise for my help!
3 Draw the spear and javelin
   against my pursuers!
Say to my soul,
   "I am your deliverance!"

4 Let them be put to shame and dishonor
   who seek after my life!
Let them be turned back and con-
   founded
   who devise evil against me!
5 Let them be like chaff before the
   wind,
   with the angel of the LORD driving them on!
6 Let their way be dark and slippery,
   with the angel of the LORD pursu-
   ing them!

7 For without cause they hid their net
   for me;
   without cause they dug a pit for
   my life.
8 Let ruin come upon them unawares!
   And let the net which they hid en-
   snare them;
   let them fall therein to ruin!
9 Then my soul shall rejoice in the
   LORD,
   exulting in his deliverance.

10 All my bones shall say,
   "O LORD, who is like thee,
   thou who deliverest the weak
   from him who is too strong for
   him,
   the weak and needy from him
   who despoils him?"

11 Malicious witnesses rise up;
   they ask me of things that I know
   not.
12 They requite me evil for good;
   my soul is forlorn.
13 But I, when they were sick—
   I wore sackcloth,
   I afflicted myself with fasting.
   I prayed with head bowed on my
   bosom,
14   as though I grieved for my friend
   or my brother;
   I went about as one who laments his
   mother,
   bowed down and in mourning.

15 But at my stumbling they gathered
   in glee,
   they gathered together against
   me;
   cripples whom I knew not
   slandered me without ceasing;
16 they impiously mocked more and
   more,
   gnashing at me with their teeth.

17 How long, O LORD, wilt thou look
   on?
   Rescue me from their ravages,
   my life from the lions!
18 Then I will thank thee in the great
   congregation;
   in the mighty throng I will praise
   thee.
19 Let not those rejoice over me
   who are wrongfully my foes,
   and let not those wink the eye
   who hate me without cause.
20 For they do not speak peace,
   but against those who are quiet in
   the land
   they conceive words of deceit.
21 They open wide their mouths
   against me;
   they say, "Aha, Aha!
   our eyes have seen it!"
22 Thou hast seen, O LORD; be not silent!
   O LORD, be not far from me!

²³Bestir thyself, and awake for my
right,
for my cause, my God and my
Lord!
²⁴Vindicate me, O LORD, my God,
according to thy righteousness;
and let them not rejoice over me!
²⁵Let them not say to themselves,
"Aha, we have our heart's desire!"
Let them not say, "We have swallowed him up."

²⁶Let them be put to shame and confusion altogether
who rejoice at my calamity!
Let them be clothed with shame and
dishonor
who magnify themselves against
me!

²⁷Let those who desire my vindication
shout for joy and be glad,
and say evermore,
"Great is the LORD,
who delights in the welfare of his
servant!"
²⁸Then my tongue shall tell of thy
righteousness
and of thy praise all the day long.

To the choirmaster. A Psalm of David,
the servant of the LORD.

36 Transgression speaks to the
wicked
deep in his heart;
there is no fear of God
before his eyes.
²For he flatters himself in his own
eyes
that his iniquity cannot be found
out and hated.
³The words of his mouth are mischief
and deceit;
he has ceased to act wisely and do
good.
⁴He plots mischief while on his bed;
he sets himself in a way that is not
good;
he spurns not evil.

⁵Thy steadfast love, O LORD, extends
to the heavens,
thy faithfulness to the clouds.

⁶Thy righteousness is like the
mountains of God,
thy judgments are like the great
deep;
man and beast thou savest, O
LORD.
⁷How precious is thy steadfast love,
O God!
The children of men take refuge in
the shadow of thy wings.
⁸They feast on the abundance of thy
house,
and thou givest them drink from
the river of thy delights.
⁹For with thee is the fountain of life;
in thy light do we see light.

¹⁰O continue thy steadfast love to
those who know thee,
and thy salvation to the upright of
heart!
¹¹Let not the foot of arrogance come
upon me,
nor the hand of the wicked drive
me away.
¹²There the evildoers lie prostrate,
they are thrust down, unable to
rise.

A Psalm of David.

37 Fret not yourself because of the
wicked,
be not envious of wrongdoers!
²For they will soon fade like the
grass,
and wither like the green herb.

³Trust in the LORD, and do good;
so you will dwell in the land, and
enjoy security.
⁴Take delight in the LORD,
and he will give you the desires of
your heart.

⁵Commit your way to the LORD;
trust in him, and he will act.
⁶He will bring forth your vindication
as the light,
and your right as the noonday.
⁷Be still before the LORD, and wait
patiently for him;
fret not yourself over him who
prospers in his way,
over the man who carries out evil
devices!

⁸Refrain from anger, and forsake
    wrath!
  Fret not yourself; it tends only to
    evil.
⁹For the wicked shall be cut off;
  but those who wait for the LORD
    shall possess the land.

¹⁰Yet a little while, and the wicked
    will be no more;
  though you look well at his place,
    he will not be there.
¹¹But the meek shall possess the land,
  and delight themselves in abun-
    dant prosperity.

¹²The wicked plots against the right-
    eous,
  and gnashes his teeth at him;
¹³but the LORD laughs at the wicked,
  for he sees that his day is coming.

¹⁴The wicked draw the sword and
    bend their bows,
  to bring down the poor and
    needy,
  to slay those who walk uprightly;
¹⁵their sword shall enter their own
    heart,
  and their bows shall be broken.

¹⁶Better is a little that the righteous
    has
  than the abundance of many
    wicked.
¹⁷For the arms of the wicked shall be
    broken;
  but the LORD upholds the right-
    eous.

¹⁸The LORD knows the days of the
    blameless,
  and their heritage will abide for
    ever;
¹⁹they are not put to shame in evil
    times,
  in the days of famine they have
    abundance.
²⁰But the wicked perish;
  the enemies of the LORD are like
    the glory of the pastures,
  they vanish—like smoke they
    vanish away.
²¹The wicked borrows, and cannot
    pay back,
  but the righteous is generous and
    gives;

²²for those blessed by the LORD shall
    possess the land,
  but those cursed by him shall be
    cut off.

²³The steps of a man are from the
    LORD,
  and he establishes him in whose
    way he delights;
²⁴though he fall, he shall not be cast
    headlong,
  for the LORD is the stay of his
    hand.

²⁵I have been young, and now am old;
  yet I have not seen the righteous
    forsaken
  or his children begging bread.
²⁶He is ever giving liberally and lend-
    ing,
  and his children become a bless-
    ing.

²⁷Depart from evil, and do good;
  so shall you abide for ever.
²⁸For the LORD loves justice;
  he will not forsake his saints.

  The righteous shall be preserved for
    ever,
  but the children of the wicked
    shall be cut off.
²⁹The righteous shall possess the land,
  and dwell upon it for ever.

³⁰The mouth of the righteous utters
    wisdom,
  and his tongue speaks justice.
³¹The law of his God is in his heart;
  his steps do not slip.

³²The wicked watches the righteous,
  and seeks to slay him.
³³The LORD will not abandon him to
    his power,
  or let him be condemned when he
    is brought to trial.

³⁴Wait for the LORD, and keep to his
    way,
  and he will exalt you to possess
    the land;
  you will look on the destruction of
    the wicked.

³⁵I have seen a wicked man overbear-
    ing,

and towering like a cedar of Lebanon.
36 Again I passed by, and, lo, he was no more;
though I sought him, he could not be found.

37 Mark the blameless man, and behold the upright,
for there is posterity for the man of peace.
38 But transgressors shall be altogether destroyed;
the posterity of the wicked shall be cut off.

39 The salvation of the righteous is from the LORD;
he is their refuge in the time of trouble.
40 The LORD helps them and delivers them;
he delivers them from the wicked, and saves them,
because they take refuge in him.

A Psalm of David, for the memorial offering.

38 O LORD, rebuke me not in thy anger,
nor chasten me in thy wrath!
2 For thy arrows have sunk into me,
and thy hand has come down on me.

3 There is no soundness in my flesh because of thy indignation;
there is no health in my bones because of my sin.
4 For my iniquities have gone over my head;
they weigh like a burden too heavy for me.

5 My wounds grow foul and fester because of my foolishness,
6 I am utterly bowed down and prostrate;
all the day I go about mourning.
7 For my loins are filled with burning,
and there is no soundness in my flesh.
8 I am utterly spent and crushed;
I groan because of the tumult of my heart.

9 Lord, all my longing is known to thee,
my sighing is not hidden from thee.
10 My heart throbs, my strength fails me;
and the light of my eyes—it also has gone from me.
11 My friends and companions stand aloof from my plague,
and my kinsmen stand afar off.
12 Those who seek my life lay their snares,
those who seek my hurt speak of ruin,
and meditate treachery all the day long.

13 But I am like a deaf man, I do not hear,
like a dumb man who does not open his mouth.
14 Yea, I am like a man who does not hear,
and in whose mouth are no rebukes.
15 But for thee, O LORD, do I wait;
it is thou, O LORD my God, who wilt answer.
16 For I pray, "Only let them not rejoice over me,
who boast against me when my foot slips!"

17 For I am ready to fall,
and my pain is ever with me.
18 I confess my iniquity,
I am sorry for my sin.
19 Those who are my foes without cause are mighty,
and many are those who hate me wrongfully.
20 Those who render me evil for good are my adversaries because I follow after good.
21 Do not forsake me, O LORD!
O my God, be not far from me!
22 Make haste to help me,
O Lord, my salvation!

To the choirmaster: to Jeduthun. A Psalm of David.

39 I said, "I will guard my ways,
that I may not sin with my tongue;

I will bridle my mouth,
so long as the wicked are in my
presence."
² I was dumb and silent,
I held my peace to no avail;
my distress grew worse,
3   my heart became hot within me.
As I mused, the fire burned;
then I spoke with my tongue:

⁴ "LORD, let me know my end,
and what is the measure of my
days;
let me know how fleeting my life
is!
⁵ Behold, thou hast made my days a
few handbreadths,
and my lifetime is as nothing in
thy sight.
Surely every man stands as a mere
breath!   *Selah*

6   Surely man goes about as a
shadow!
Surely for nought are they in tur-
moil;
man heaps up, and knows not
who will gather!

⁷ "And now, Lord, for what do I wait?
My hope is in thee.
⁸ Deliver me from all my transgressions.
Make me not the scorn of the fool!

⁹ I am dumb, I do not open my
mouth;
for it is thou who hast done it.
¹⁰ Remove thy stroke from me;
I am spent by the blows of thy
hand.
¹¹ When thou dost chasten man
with rebukes for sin,
thou dost consume like a moth what
is dear to him;
surely every man is a mere breath!
Selah

¹² "Hear my prayer, O LORD,
and give ear to my cry;
hold not thy peace at my tears!
For I am thy passing guest,
a sojourner, like all my fathers.

¹³ Look away from me, that I may
know gladness,
before I depart and be no more!"

To the choirmaster. A Psalm of David.

40 I waited patiently for the LORD;
he inclined to me and heard my
cry.
² He drew me up from the desolate
pit,
out of the miry bog,
and set my feet upon a rock,
making my steps secure.
³ He put a new song in my mouth,
a song of praise to our God.
Many will see and fear,
and put their trust in the LORD.

⁴ Blessed is the man who makes
the LORD his trust,
who does not turn to the proud,
to those who go astray after false
gods!

⁵ Thou hast multiplied, O LORD my
God,
thy wondrous deeds and thy
thoughts toward us;
none can compare with thee!
Were I to proclaim and tell of them,
they would be more than can be
numbered.

⁶ Sacrifice and offering thou dost not
desire;
but thou hast given me an open
ear.
Burnt offering and sin offering
thou hast not required.
⁷ Then I said, "Lo, I come;
in the roll of the book it is written
of me;
⁸ I delight to do thy will, O my God;
thy law is within my heart."

⁹ I have told the glad news of deliverance
in the great congregation;
lo, I have not restrained my lips,
as thou knowest, O LORD.
¹⁰ I have not hid thy saving help
within my heart,
I have spoken of thy faithfulness
and thy salvation;
I have not concealed thy steadfast
love and thy faithfulness
from the great congregation.

¹¹ Do not thou, O LORD, withhold
thy mercy from me,

let thy steadfast love and thy faithfulness
ever preserve me!
¹²For evils have encompassed me
without number;
my iniquities have overtaken me,
till I cannot see;
they are more than the hairs of my
head;
my heart fails me.

¹³Be pleased, O LORD, to deliver me!
O LORD, make haste to help me!
¹⁴Let them be put to shame and confusion altogether
who seek to snatch away my life;
let them be turned back and brought
to dishonor
who desire my hurt!
¹⁵Let them be appalled because of
their shame
who say to me, "Aha, Aha!"

¹⁶But may all who seek thee
rejoice and be glad in thee;
may those who love thy salvation
say continually, "Great is the
LORD!"
¹⁷As for me, I am poor and needy;
but the Lord takes thought for me.
Thou art my help and my deliverer;
do not tarry, O my God!

To the choirmaster. A Psalm of David.

41 Blessed is he who considers the
poor!
The LORD delivers him in the day
of trouble;
²the LORD protects him and keeps
him alive;
he is called blessed in the land;
thou dost not give him up to the
will of his enemies.
³The LORD sustains him on his sick-
bed;
in his illness thou healest all his
infirmities.

⁴As for me, I said, "O LORD, be gracious to me;
heal me, for I have sinned against
thee!"
⁵My enemies say of me in malice:
"When will he die, and his name
perish?"

⁶And when one comes to see me, he
utters empty words,
while his heart gathers mischief;
when he goes out, he tells it
abroad.
⁷All who hate me whisper together
about me;
they imagine the worst for me.
⁸They say, "A deadly thing has fas-
tened upon him;
he will not rise again from where
he lies."
⁹Even my bosom friend in whom I
trusted,
who ate of my bread, has lifted his
heel against me.
¹⁰But do thou, O LORD, be gracious to
me,
and raise me up, that I may requite them!

¹¹By this I know that thou art pleased
with me,
in that my enemy has not tri-
umphed over me.
¹²But thou hast upheld me because of
my integrity,
and set me in thy presence for
ever.

¹³Blessed be the LORD, the God of Israel,
from everlasting to everlasting!
Amen and Amen.

BOOK II

To the choirmaster. A Maskil of the
Sons of Korah.

42 As a hart longs
for flowing streams,
so longs my soul
for thee, O God.
²My soul thirsts for God,
for the living God.
When shall I come and behold
the face of God?
³My tears have been my food
day and night,
while men say to me continually,
"Where is your God?"
⁴These things I remember,
as I pour out my soul:

how I went with the throng,
and led them in procession to the
house of God,
with glad shouts and songs of
thanksgiving,
a multitude keeping festival.
5 Why are you cast down, O my soul,
and why are you disquieted
within me?
Hope in God; for I shall again praise
him,
my help 6and my God.

My soul is cast down within me,
therefore I remember thee
from the land of Jordan and of Hermon,
from Mount Mizar.
7 Deep calls to deep
at the thunder of thy cataracts;
all thy waves and thy billows
have gone over me.
8 By day the LORD commands his
steadfast love;
and at night his song is with me,
a prayer to the God of my life.

9 I say to God, my rock:
"Why hast thou forgotten me?
Why go I mourning
because of the oppression of the
enemy?"
10 As with a deadly wound in my
body,
my adversaries taunt me,
while they say to me continually,
"Where is your God?"

11 Why are you cast down, O my soul,
and why are you disquieted
within me?
Hope in God; for I shall again praise
him,
my help and my God.

43 Vindicate me, O God, and defend my cause
against an ungodly people;
from deceitful and unjust men
deliver me!
2 For thou art the God in whom I take
refuge;
why hast thou cast me off?
Why go I mourning
because of the oppression of the
enemy?

3 Oh send out thy light and thy truth;
let them lead me,
let them bring me to thy holy hill
and to thy dwelling!
4 Then I will go to the altar of God,
to God my exceeding joy;
and I will praise thee with the lyre,
O God, my God.

5 Why are you cast down, O my soul,
and why are you disquieted
within me?
Hope in God; for I shall again praise
him,
my help and my God.

To the choirmaster. A Maskil of the
Sons of Korah.

44 We have heard with our ears, O
God,
our fathers have told us,
what deeds thou didst perform in
their days,
in the days of old:
2 thou with thy own hand didst drive
out the nations,
but them thou didst plant;
thou didst afflict the peoples,
but them thou didst set free;
3 for not by their own sword did they
win the land,
nor did their own arm give them
victory;
but thy right hand, and thy arm,
and the light of thy countenance;
for thou didst delight in them.

4 Thou art my King and my God,
who ordainest victories for Jacob.
5 Through thee we push down our
foes;
through thy name we tread down
our assailants.
6 For not in my bow do I trust,
nor can my sword save me.
7 But thou hast saved us from our
foes,
and hast put to confusion those
who hate us.
8 In God we have boasted continually,
and we will give thanks to thy
name for ever.   *Selah*

9 Yet thou hast cast us off and abased
us,

and hast not gone out with our
armies.
[10]Thou hast made us turn back from
the foe;
and our enemies have gotten
spoil.
[11]Thou hast made us like sheep for
slaughter,
and hast scattered us among the
nations.
[12]Thou hast sold thy people for a
trifle,
demanding no high price for
them.

[13]Thou hast made us the taunt of our
neighbors,
the derision and scorn of those
about us.
[14]Thou hast made us a byword among
the nations,
a laughingstock among the
peoples.
[15]All day long my disgrace is before
me,
and shame has covered my face,
[16]at the words of the taunters and re-
vilers,
at the sight of the enemy and the
avenger.

[17]All this has come upon us,
though we have not forgotten
thee,
or been false to thy covenant.
[18]Our heart has not turned back,
nor have our steps departed from
thy way,
[19]that thou shouldst have broken us in
the place of jackals,
and covered us with deep darkness.

[20]If we had forgotten the name of our
God,
or spread forth our hands to a
strange god,
[21]would not God discover this?
For he knows the secrets of the
heart.
[22]Nay, for thy sake we are slain all the
day long,
and accounted as sheep for the
slaughter.

[23]Rouse thyself! Why sleepest thou, O
Lord!
Awake! Do not cast us off for ever!
[24]Why dost thou hide thy face?
Why dost thou forget our affliction and oppression?
[25]For our soul is bowed down to the
dust;
our body cleaves to the ground.
[26]Rise up, come to our help!
Deliver us for the sake of thy
steadfast love!

To the choirmaster: according to
Lilies. A Maskil of the Sons of Korah;
a love song.

45

My heart overflows with a
goodly theme,
I address my verses to the king;
my tongue is like the pen of a
ready scribe.

[2]You are the fairest of the sons of
men;
grace is poured upon your lips;
therefore God has blessed you for
ever.
[3]Gird your sword upon your thigh, O
mighty one,
in your glory and majesty!

[4]In your majesty ride forth victori-
ously
for the cause of truth and to defend the right;
let your right hand teach you
dread deeds!
[5]Your arrows are sharp
in the heart of the king's enemies;
the peoples fall under you.

[6]Your divine throne endures for ever
and ever.
Your royal scepter is a scepter of
equity;
[7] you love righteousness and hate
wickedness.
Therefore God, your God, has
anointed you
with the oil of gladness above
your fellows;
[8] your robes are all fragrant with
myrrh and aloes and cassia.
From ivory palaces stringed instruments make you glad;
[9] daughters of kings are among
your ladies of honor;

at your right hand stands the queen in gold of Ophir.

¹⁰Hear, O daughter, consider, and incline your ear;
forget your people and your father's house;
¹¹ and the king will desire your beauty.
Since he is your lord, bow to him;
¹² the people of Tyre will sue your favor with gifts,
the richest of the people ¹³with all kinds of wealth.
The princess is decked in her chamber with gold-woven robes;

¹⁴ in many-colored robes she is led to the king,
with her virgin companions, her escort, in her train.
¹⁵With joy and gladness they are led along
as they enter the palace of the king.

¹⁶Instead of your fathers shall be your sons;
you will make them princes in all the earth.
¹⁷I will cause your name to be celebrated in all generations;
therefore the peoples will praise you for ever and ever.

To the choirmaster. A Psalm of the Sons of Korah. According to Alamoth. A Song.

46 God is our refuge and strength,
a very present help in trouble.
² Therefore we will not fear though the earth should change,
though the mountains shake in the heart of the sea;
³ though its waters roar and foam,
though the mountains tremble with its tumult.   *Selah*

⁴ There is a river whose streams make glad the city of God,
the holy habitation of the Most High.
⁵ God is in the midst of her, she shall not be moved;
God will help her right early.

⁶ The nations rage, the kingdoms totter;
he utters his voice, the earth melts.
⁷ The LORD of hosts is with us;
the God of Jacob is our refuge.   *Selah*

⁸ Come, behold the works of the LORD,
how he has wrought desolations in the earth.
⁹ He makes wars cease to the end of the earth;
he breaks the bow, and shatters the spear,
he burns the chariots with fire!
¹⁰ "Be still, and know that I am God.
I am exalted among the nations,
I am exalted in the earth!"
¹¹ The LORD of hosts is with us;
the God of Jacob is our refuge.   *Selah*

To the choirmaster. A Psalm of the Sons of Korah.

47 Clap your hands, all peoples!
Shout to God with loud songs of joy!
² For the LORD, the Most High, is terrible,
a great king over all the earth.
³ He subdued peoples under us,
and nations under our feet.
⁴ He chose our heritage for us,
the pride of Jacob whom he loves.   *Selah*

⁵ God has gone up with a shout,
the LORD with the sound of a trumpet.
⁶ Sing praises to God, sing praises!
Sing praises to our King, sing praises!
⁷ For God is the king of all the earth;
sing praises with a psalm!

⁸ God reigns over the nations;
God sits on his holy throne.
⁹ The princes of the peoples gather
as the people of the God of Abraham.
For the shields of the earth belong to God;
he is highly exalted!

A Song. A Psalm of the Sons of Korah.

48 Great is the LORD and greatly to be praised
in the city of our God!
His holy mountain, ²beautiful in elevation,
is the joy of all the earth,
Mount Zion, in the far north,
the city of the great King.
³Within her citadels God
has shown himself a sure defense.

⁴For lo, the kings assembled,
they came on together.
⁵As soon as they saw it, they were astounded,
they were in panic, they took to flight;
⁶trembling took hold of them there,
anguish as of a woman in travail.
⁷By the east wind thou didst shatter
the ships of Tarshish.
⁸As we have heard, so have we seen
in the city of the LORD of hosts,
in the city of our God,
which God establishes for ever.
Selah

⁹We have thought on thy steadfast love, O God,
in the midst of thy temple.
¹⁰As thy name, O God,
so thy praise reaches to the ends of the earth.
Thy right hand is filled with victory;
¹¹ let Mount Zion be glad!
Let the daughters of Judah rejoice
because of thy judgments!

¹²Walk about Zion, go round about her,
number her towers,
¹³consider well her ramparts,
go through her citadels;
that you may tell the next generation
¹⁴ that this is God,
our God for ever and ever.
He will be our guide for ever.

To the choirmaster. A Psalm of the Sons of Korah.

49 Hear this, all peoples!
Give ear, all inhabitants of the world,

²both low and high,
rich and poor together!
³My mouth shall speak wisdom;
the meditation of my heart shall be understanding.
⁴I will incline my ear to a proverb;
I will solve my riddle to the music of the lyre.

⁵Why should I fear in times of trouble,
when the iniquity of my persecutors surrounds me,
⁶men who trust in their wealth
and boast of the abundance of their riches?
⁷Truly no man can ransom himself,
or give to God the price of his life,
⁸for the ransom of his life is costly,
and can never suffice,
⁹that he should continue to live on for ever,
and never see the Pit.
¹⁰Yea, he shall see that even the wise die,
the fool and the stupid alike must perish
and leave their wealth to others.
¹¹Their graves are their homes for ever,
their dwelling places to all generations,
though they named lands their own.
¹²Man cannot abide in his pomp,
he is like the beasts that perish.

¹³This is the fate of those who have foolish confidence,
the end of those who are pleased with their portion. *Selah*
¹⁴Like sheep they are appointed for Sheol;
Death shall be their shepherd;
straight to the grave they descend,
and their form shall waste away;
Sheol shall be their home.
¹⁵But God will ransom my soul from the power of Sheol,
for he will receive me. *Selah*

¹⁶Be not afraid when one becomes rich,
when the glory of his house increases.
¹⁷For when he dies he will carry nothing away;

his glory will not go down after
him.
¹⁸ Though, while he lives, he counts
himself happy,
and though a man gets praise
when he does well for himself,
¹⁹ he will go to the generation of his
fathers,
who will never more see the light.
²⁰ Man cannot abide in his pomp,
he is like the beasts that perish.

A Psalm of Asaph.

50 The Mighty One, God the
LORD,
speaks and summons the earth
from the rising of the sun to its
setting.
² Out of Zion, the perfection of
beauty,
God shines forth.

³ Our God comes, he does not keep
silence,
before him is a devouring fire,
round about him a mighty tempest.
⁴ He calls to the heavens above
and to the earth, that he may
judge his people:
⁵ "Gather to me my faithful ones,
who made a covenant with me by
sacrifice!"
⁶ The heavens declare his righteousness,
for God himself is judge!   *Selah*

⁷ "Hear, O my people, and I will
speak,
O Israel, I will testify against you.
I am God, your God.
⁸ I do not reprove you for your sacrifices;
your burnt offerings are continually before me.
⁹ I will accept no bull from your
house,
nor he-goat from your folds.
¹⁰ For every beast of the forest is mine,
the cattle on a thousand hills.
¹¹ I know all the birds of the air,
and all that moves in the field is
mine.
¹² If I were hungry, I would not tell
you;

for the world and all that is in it is
mine.
¹³ Do I eat the flesh of bulls,
or drink the blood of goats?
¹⁴ Offer to God a sacrifice of thanksgiving,
and pay your vows to the Most
High;
¹⁵ and call upon me in the day of trouble;
I will deliver you, and you shall
glorify me."

¹⁶ But to the wicked God says:
"What right have you to recite my
statutes,
or take my covenant on your lips?
¹⁷ For you hate discipline,
and you cast my words behind
you.
¹⁸ If you see a thief, you are a friend of
his;
and you keep company with adul-
terers.
¹⁹ You give your mouth free rein for
evil,
and your tongue frames deceit.
²⁰ You sit and speak against your
brother;
you slander your own mother's
son.
²¹ These things you have done and I
have been silent;
you thought that I was one like
yourself.
But now I rebuke you, and lay the
charge before you.

²² "Mark this, then, you who forget
God,
lest I rend, and there be none to
deliver!
²³ He who brings thanksgiving as his
sacrifice honors me;
to him who orders his way aright
I will show the salvation of God!"

To the choirmaster. A Psalm of David,
when Nathan the prophet came to
him, after he had gone in to
Bathsheba.

51 Have mercy on me, O God,
according to thy steadfast love;
according to thy abundant mercy
blot out my transgressions.

2 Wash me thoroughly from my iniquity,
and cleanse me from my sin!

3 For I know my transgressions,
and my sin is ever before me.
4 Against thee, thee only, have I
sinned,
and done that which is evil in thy
sight,
so that thou art justified in thy
sentence
and blameless in thy judgment.
5 Behold, I was brought forth in
iniquity,
and in sin did my mother conceive me.

6 Behold, thou desirest truth in the
inward being;
therefore teach me wisdom in my
secret heart.

7 Purge me with hyssop, and I shall
be clean;
wash me, and I shall be whiter
than snow.
8 Fill me with joy and gladness;
let the bones which thou hast
broken rejoice.
9 Hide thy face from my sins,
and blot out all my iniquities.

10 Create in me a clean heart, O God,
and put a new and right spirit
within me.
11 Cast me not away from thy presence,
and take not thy holy Spirit from
me.
12 Restore to me the joy of thy salvation,
and uphold me with a willing
spirit.

13 Then I will teach transgressors thy
ways,
and sinners will return to thee.
14 Deliver me from bloodguiltiness, O
God,
thou God of my salvation,
and my tongue will sing aloud of
thy deliverance.

15 O Lord, open thou my lips,
and my mouth shall show forth
thy praise.

16 For thou hast no delight in sacrifice;
were I to give a burnt offering,
thou wouldst not be pleased.
17 The sacrifice acceptable to God is a
broken spirit;
a broken and contrite heart, O
God, thou wilt not despise.

18 Do good to Zion in thy good pleasure;
rebuild the walls of Jerusalem,
19 then wilt thou delight in right sacrifices,
in burnt offerings and whole
burnt offerings;
then bulls will be offered on thy
altar.

To the choirmaster. A Maskil of David,
when Doeg, the Edomite, came and
told Saul, "David has come to the
house of Ahimelech."

52 Why do you boast, O mighty
man,
of mischief done against the
godly?
All the day 2 you are plotting destruction.
Your tongue is like a sharp razor,
you worker of treachery.
3 You love evil more than good,
and lying more than speaking the
truth.   Selah
4 You love all words that devour,
O deceitful tongue.

5 But God will break you down for
ever;
he will snatch and tear you from
your tent;
he will uproot you from the land
of the living.   Selah
6 The righteous shall see, and fear,
and shall laugh at him, saying,
7 "See the man who would not make
God his refuge,
but trusted in the abundance of his
riches,
and sought refuge in his wealth!"

8 But I am like a green olive tree in
the house of God.
I trust in the steadfast love of God
for ever and ever.

⁹I will thank thee for ever,
   because thou hast done it.
I will proclaim thy name, for it is
   good,
   in the presence of the godly.

To the choirmaster: according to
Mahalath. A Maskil of David.

53 The fool says in his heart,
   "There is no God."
They are corrupt, doing abominable
   iniquity;
   there is none that does good.
² God looks down from heaven
   upon the sons of men
to see if there are any that are wise,
   that seek after God.

³ They have all fallen away;
   they are all alike depraved;
there is none that does good,
   no, not one.

⁴ Have those who work evil no understanding,
   who eat up my people as they eat
   bread,
   and do not call upon God?

⁵ There they are, in great terror,
   in terror such as has not been!
For God will scatter the bones of the
   ungodly;
   they will be put to shame, for God
   has rejected them.

⁶ O that deliverance for Israel would
   come from Zion!
   When God restores the fortunes of
   his people,
Jacob will rejoice and Israel be glad.

To the choirmaster: with stringed instruments. A Maskil of David, when
the Ziphites went and told Saul,
   "David is in hiding among us."

54 Save me, O God, by thy name,
   and vindicate me by thy might.
² Hear my prayer, O God;
   give ear to the words of my
   mouth.
³ For insolent men have risen against
   me,

ruthless men seek my life;
   they do not set God before them.
                              Selah

⁴ Behold, God is my helper;
   the LORD is the upholder of my
   life.
⁵ He will requite my enemies with
   evil;
   in thy faithfulness put an end to
   them.

⁶ With a freewill offering I will sacrifice to thee;
   I will give thanks to thy name, O
   LORD, for it is good.
⁷ For thou hast delivered me from
   every trouble,
   and my eye has looked in triumph
   on my enemies.

To the choirmaster: with stringed instruments. A Maskil of David.

55 Give ear to my prayer, O God;
   and hide not thyself from my
   supplication!
² Attend to me, and answer me;
   I am overcome by my trouble.
I am distraught ³by the noise of the
   enemy,
   because of the oppression of the
   wicked.
For they bring trouble upon me,
   and in anger they cherish enmity
   against me.

⁴ My heart is in anguish within me,
   the terrors of death have fallen
   upon me.
⁵ Fear and trembling come upon me,
   and horror overwhelms me.
⁶ And I say, "O that I had wings like a
   dove!
   I would fly away and be at rest;
⁷ yea, I would wander afar,
   I would lodge in the wilderness,
                              Selah
⁸ I would haste to find me a shelter
   from the raging wind and tempest."

⁹ Destroy their plans, O Lord, confuse
   their tongues;
   for I see violence and strife in the
   city.

[10]Day and night they go around it on
its walls;
and mischief and trouble are within
it,
[11] ruin is in its midst;
oppression and fraud
do not depart from its market
place.

[12]It is not an enemy who taunts me—
then I could bear it;
it is not an adversary who deals insolently with me—
then I could hide from him.
[13]But it is you, my equal,
my companion, my familiar
friend.
[14]We used to hold sweet converse together;
within God's house we walked in
fellowship.

[15]Let death come upon them;
let them go down to Sheol alive;
let them go away in terror into
their graves.

[16]But I call upon God;
and the LORD will save me.
[17]Evening and morning and at noon
I utter my complaint and moan,
and he will hear my voice.
[18]He will deliver my soul in safety
from the battle that I wage,
for many are arrayed against me.
[19]God will give ear, and humble them,
he who is enthroned from of old;
because they keep no law,
and do not fear God.   *Selah*

[20]My companion stretched out his
hand against his friends,
he violated his covenant.
[21]His speech was smoother than but-
ter,
yet war was in his heart;
his words were softer than oil,
yet they were drawn swords.

[22]Cast your burden on the LORD,
and he will sustain you;
he will never permit
the righteous to be moved.

[23]But thou, O God, wilt cast them
down
into the lowest pit;

men of blood and treachery
shall not live out half their days.
But I will trust in thee.

To the choirmaster: according to The
Dove on Far-off Terebinths. A Miktam
of David, when the Philistines seized
him in Gath.

56 Be gracious to me, O God,
for men trample upon me;
all day long foemen oppress me;
[2]my enemies trample upon me all
day long,
for many fight against me
proudly.
[3]When I am afraid,
I put my trust in thee.
[4]In God, whose word I praise,
in God I trust without a fear.
What can flesh do to me?

[5]All day long they seek to injure my
cause;
all their thoughts are against me
for evil.
[6]They band themselves together,
they lurk,
they watch my steps.
As they have waited for my life,
[7] so recompense them for their
crime;
in wrath cast down the peoples, O
God!
[8]Thou hast kept count of my toss-
ings;
put thou my tears in thy bottle!
Are they not in thy book?
[9]Then my enemies will be turned
back
in the day when I call.
This I know, that God is for me.
[10]In God, whose word I praise,
in the LORD, whose word I praise,
[11]in God I trust without a fear.
What can man do to me?

[12]My vows to thee I must perform, O
God;
I will render thank offerings to
thee.
[13]For thou hast delivered my soul
from death,
yea, my feet from falling,
that I may walk before God
in the light of life.

To the choirmaster: according to Do Not Destroy. A Miktam of David, when he fled from Saul, in the cave.

57 Be merciful to me, O God,
be merciful to me,
for in thee my soul takes refuge;
in the shadow of thy wings I will take refuge,
till the storms of destruction pass by.
2 I cry to God Most High,
to God who fulfils his purpose for me.
3 He will send from heaven and save me,
he will put to shame those who trample upon me.   *Selah*
God will send forth his steadfast love and his faithfulness!
4 I lie in the midst of lions
that greedily devour the sons of men;
their teeth are spears and arrows,
their tongues sharp swords.
5 Be exalted, O God, above the heavens!
Let thy glory be over all the earth!

6 They set a net for my steps;
my soul was bowed down.
They dug a pit in my way,
but they have fallen into it themselves.   *Selah*
7 My heart is steadfast, O God,
my heart is steadfast!
I will sing and make melody!
8   Awake, my soul!
Awake, O harp and lyre!
I will awake the dawn!
9 I will give thanks to thee, O Lord,
among the peoples,
I will sing praises to thee among the nations.
10 For thy steadfast love is great to the heavens,
thy faithfulness to the clouds.
11 Be exalted, O God, above the heavens!
Let thy glory be over all the earth!

To the choirmaster: according to Do Not Destroy. A Miktam of David.

58 Do you indeed decree what is right, you gods?

Do you judge the sons of men uprightly?
2 Nay, in your hearts you devise wrongs;
your hands deal out violence on earth.
3 The wicked go astray from the womb,
they err from their birth, speaking lies.
4 They have venom like the venom of a serpent,
like the deaf adder that stops its ear,
5 so that it does not hear the voice of charmers
or of the cunning enchanter.

6 O God, break the teeth in their mouths;
tear out the fangs of the young lions, O LORD!
7 Let them vanish like water that runs away;
like grass let them be trodden down and wither.
8 Let them be like the snail which dissolves into slime,
like the untimely birth that never sees the sun.
9 Sooner than your pots can feel the heat of thorns,
whether green or ablaze, may he sweep them away!
10 The righteous will rejoice when he sees the vengeance;
he will bathe his feet in the blood of the wicked.
11 Men will say, "Surely there is a reward for the righteous;
surely there is a God who judges on earth."

To the choirmaster: according to Do Not Destroy. A Miktam of David, when Saul sent men to watch his house in order to kill him.

59 Deliver me from my enemies, O my God,
protect me from those who rise up against me,
2 deliver me from those who work evil,
and save me from bloodthirsty men.

3 For, lo, they lie in wait for my life;
    fierce men band themselves
    against me.
  For no transgression or sin of mine,
    O LORD,
4   for no fault of mine, they run and
    make ready.
  Rouse thyself, come to my help, and
    see!
5   Thou, LORD God of hosts, art God
    of Israel.
  Awake to punish all the nations;
    spare none of those who treacher-
    ously plot evil.   *Selah*
6 Each evening they come back,
    howling like dogs
    and prowling about the city.
7 There they are, bellowing with their
    mouths,
    and snarling with their lips—
    for "Who," they think, "will hear
    us?"

8 But thou, O LORD, dost laugh at
    them;
    thou dost hold all the nations in
    derision.
9 O my Strength, I will sing praises to
    thee;
    for thou, O God, art my fortress.
10 My God in his steadfast love will
    meet me;
    my God will let me look in
    triumph on my enemies.

11 Slay them not, lest my people forget;
    make them totter by thy power,
    and bring them down,
  O Lord, our shield!
12 For the sin of their mouths, the
    words of their lips,
    let them be trapped in their pride.
  For the cursing and lies which they
    utter,
13   consume them in wrath,
    consume them till they are no
    more,
  that men may know that God rules
    over Jacob
  to the ends of the earth.   *Selah*

14 Each evening they come back,
    howling like dogs
    and prowling about the city.
15 They roam about for food,
    and growl if they do not get their
    fill.

16 But I will sing of thy might;
    I will sing aloud of thy steadfast
    love in the morning.
  For thou hast been to me a fortress
    and a refuge in the day of my dis-
    tress.
17 O my Strength, I will sing praises to
    thee,
    for thou, O God, art my fortress,
    the God who shows me steadfast
    love.

To the choirmaster: according to
Shushan Eduth. A Miktam of David;
for instruction; when he strove with
Aram-naharaim and with Aram-
zobah, and when Joab on his return
killed twelve thousand of Edom in the
Valley of Salt.

60 O God, thou hast rejected us,
    broken our defenses;
    thou hast been angry; oh, restore
    us,
2 Thou hast made the land to quake,
    thou hast rent it open;
    repair its breaches, for it totters.
3 Thou hast made thy people suffer
    hard things;
    thou hast given us wine to drink
    that made us reel.
4 Thou hast set up a banner for those
    who fear thee,
    to rally to it from the bow.   *Selah*
5 That thy beloved may be delivered,
    give victory by thy right hand and
    answer us!

6 God has spoken in his sanctuary:
    "With exultation I will divide up
    Shechem
    and portion out the Vale of Suc-
    coth.
7 Gilead is mine; Manas'seh is mine;
    E'phraim is my helmet;
    Judah is my scepter.
8 Moab is my washbasin;
    upon Edom I cast my shoe;
    over Philistia I shout in triumph."

9 Who will bring me to the fortified
    city?
  Who will lead me to Edom?
10 Hast thou not rejected us, O God?
    Thou dost not go forth, O God,
    with our armies.

11 O grant us help against the foe,
    for vain is the help of man!
12 With God we shall do valiantly;
    it is he who will tread down our
      foes.

To the choirmaster: with stringed instruments. A Psalm of David.

61 Hear my cry, O God,
    listen to my prayer;
2 from the end of the earth I call to
    thee,
    when my heart is faint.
Lead thou me
    to the rock that is higher than I;
3 for thou art my refuge,
    a strong tower against the enemy.
4 Let me dwell in thy tent for ever!
    Oh to be safe under the shelter of
      thy wings!   *Selah*
5 For thou, O God, hast heard my
    vows,
    thou hast given me the heritage of
      those who fear thy name.
6 Prolong the life of the king;
    may his years endure to all generations!
7 May he be enthroned for ever before
    God;
    bid steadfast love and faithfulness
      watch over him!
8 So will I ever sing praises to thy
    name,
    as I pay my vows day after day.

To the choirmaster: according to Jeduthun. A Psalm of David.

62 For God alone my soul waits in
    silence;
    from him comes my salvation.
2 He only is my rock and my salvation,
    my fortress; I shall not be greatly
      moved.
3 How long will you set upon a man
    to shatter him, all of you,
    like a leaning wall, a tottering
      fence?
4 They only plan to thrust him down
    from his eminence.
They take pleasure in falsehood.
They bless with their mouths,
    but inwardly they curse.   *Selah*

5 For God alone my soul waits in silence,
    for my hope is from him.
6 He only is my rock and my salvation,
    my fortress; I shall not be shaken.
7 On God rests my deliverance and
    my honor;
    my mighty rock, my refuge is
      God.

8 Trust in him at all times, O people;
    pour out your heart before him;
    God is a refuge for us.   *Selah*

9 Men of low estate are but a breath,
    men of high estate are a delusion;
    in the balances they go up;
    they are together lighter than a
      breath.
10 Put no confidence in extortion,
    set no vain hopes on robbery;
    if riches increase, set not your
      heart on them.

11 Once God has spoken;
    twice have I heard this:
that power belongs to God;
12   and that to thee, O Lord, belongs
    steadfast love.
For thou dost requite a man
    according to his work.

A Psalm of David, when he was in the Wilderness of Judah.

63 O God, thou art my God, I seek
    thee,
    my soul thirsts for thee;
    my flesh faints for thee,
    as in a dry and weary land where
      no water is.
2 So I have looked upon thee in the
    sanctuary,
    beholding thy power and glory.
3 Because thy steadfast love is better
    than life,
    my lips will praise thee.
4 So I will bless thee as long as I live;
    I will lift up my hands and call on
      thy name.

5 My soul is feasted as with marrow
    and fat,
    and my mouth praises thee with
      joyful lips,

⁶when I think of thee upon my bed,
    and meditate on thee in the
    watches of the night;
⁷for thou hast been my help,
    and in the shadow of thy wings I
    sing for joy.
⁸My soul clings to thee;
    thy right hand upholds me.
⁹But those who seek to destroy my
    life
    shall go down into the depths of
    the earth;
¹⁰they shall be given over to the
    power of the sword,
    they shall be prey for jackals.
¹¹But the king shall rejoice in God;
    all who swear by him shall glory;
    for the mouths of liars will be
    stopped.

To the choirmaster. A Psalm of David.

64 Hear my voice, O God, in my
    complaint;
    preserve my life from dread of the
    enemy,
²hide me from the secret plots of the
    wicked,
    from the scheming of evildoers,
³who whet their tongues like swords,
    who aim bitter swords like ar-
    rows,
⁴shooting from ambush at the blame-
    less,
    shooting at him suddenly and
    without fear.
⁵They hold fast to their evil purpose;
    they talk of laying snares secretly,
    thinking, "Who can see us?
⁶ Who can search out our crimes?
    We have thought out a cunningly
    conceived plot."
    For the inward mind and heart of
    a man are deep!

⁷But God will shoot his arrow at
    them;
    they will be wounded suddenly.
⁸Because of their tongue he will bring
    them to ruin;
    all who see them will wag their
    heads.
⁹Then all men will fear;
    they will tell what God has
    wrought,
    and ponder what he has done.

¹⁰Let the righteous rejoice in the
    LORD, and take refuge in him!
    Let all the upright in heart glory!

To the choirmaster. A Psalm of David.
A Song.

65 Praise is due to thee,
    O God, in Zion;
    and to thee shall vows be per-
    formed,
² O thou who hearest prayer!
    To thee shall all flesh come
³ on account of sins.
    When our transgressions prevail
    over us,
    thou dost forgive them.
⁴Blessed is he whom thou dost
    choose and bring near,
    to dwell in thy courts!
    We shall be satisfied with the good-
    ness of thy house,
    thy holy temple!

⁵By dread deeds thou dost answer us
    with deliverance,
    O God of our salvation,
    who art the hope of all the ends of
    the earth,
    and of the farthest seas;
⁶who by thy strength hast estab-
    lished the mountains,
    being girded with might;
⁷who dost still the roaring of the seas,
    the roaring of their waves,
    the tumult of the peoples;
⁸so that those who dwell at earth's
    farthest bounds
    are afraid at thy signs;
    thou makest the outgoings of the
    morning and the evening
    to shout for joy.

⁹Thou visitest the earth and waterest
    it,
    thou greatly enrichest it;
    the river of God is full of water;
    thou providest their grain,
    for so thou hast prepared it.
¹⁰Thou waterest its furrows abun-
    dantly,
    settling its ridges,
    softening it with showers,
    and blessing its growth.
¹¹Thou crownest the year with thy
    bounty;

the tracks of thy chariot drip with
fatness.
¹²The pastures of the wilderness drip,
the hills gird themselves with joy,
¹³the meadows clothe themselves
with flocks,
the valleys deck themselves with
grain,
they shout and sing together for
joy.

To the choirmaster. A Song. A Psalm.

66 Make a joyful noise to God,
all the earth;
² sing the glory of his name;
give to him glorious praise!
³ Say to God, "How terrible are thy
deeds!
So great is thy power that thy
enemies cringe before thee.
⁴ All the earth worships thee;
they sing praises to thee,
sing praises to thy name." *Selah*

⁵ Come and see what God has done:
he is terrible in his deeds among
men.
⁶ He turned the sea into dry land;
men passed through the river on
foot.
There did we rejoice in him,
⁷ who rules by his might for ever,
whose eyes keep watch on the nations—
let not the rebellious exalt themselves. *Selah*
⁸ Bless our God, O peoples,
let the sound of his praise be
heard,
⁹ who has kept us among the living,
and has not let our feet slip.
¹⁰For thou, O God, hast tested us;
thou hast tried us as silver is tried.
¹¹Thou didst bring us into the net;
thou didst lay affliction on our
loins;
¹²thou didst let men ride over our
heads;
we went through fire and through
water;
yet thou hast brought us forth to a
spacious place.

¹³I will come into thy house with
burnt offerings;

I will pay thee my vows,
¹⁴that which my lips uttered
and my mouth promised when I
was in trouble.
¹⁵I will offer to thee burnt offerings of
fatlings,
with the smoke of the sacrifice of
rams;
I will make an offering of bulls and
goats. *Selah*

¹⁶Come and hear, all you who fear
God,
and I will tell what he has done for
me.
¹⁷I cried aloud to him,
and he was extolled with my
tongue.
¹⁸If I had cherished iniquity in my
heart,
the LORD would not have listened.
¹⁹But truly God has listened;
he has given heed to the voice of
my prayer.
²⁰Blessed be God,
because he has not rejected my
prayer
or removed his steadfast love from
me!

To the choirmaster: with stringed instruments. A Psalm. A Song.

67 May God be gracious to us and
bless us
and make his face to shine upon
us, *Selah*
² that thy way may be known upon
earth,
thy saving power among all nations.
³ Let the peoples praise thee, O God;
let all the peoples praise thee!

⁴ Let the nations be glad and sing for
joy,
for thou dost judge the peoples
with equity
and guide the nations upon earth.
Selah
⁵ Let the peoples praise thee, O God;
let all the peoples praise thee!

⁶ The earth has yielded its increase;
God, our God, has blessed us.

⁷God has blessed us;
    let all the ends of the earth fear
        him!

To the choirmaster. A Psalm of David.
A Song.

68 Let God arise, let his enemies
    be scattered;
    let those who hate him flee before
        him!
² As smoke is driven away, so drive
    them away;
    as wax melts before fire,
    let the wicked perish before God!
³ But let the righteous be joyful;
    let them exult before God;
    let them be jubilant with joy!

⁴Sing to God, sing praises to his
    name;
    lift up a song to him who rides
        upon the clouds;
    his name is the LORD, exult before
        him!
⁵ Father of the fatherless and protector
    of widows
    is God in his holy habitation.
⁶God gives the desolate a home to
    dwell in;
    he leads out the prisoners to pros-
        perity;
    but the rebellious dwell in a
        parched land.

⁷O God, when thou didst go forth
    before thy people,
    when thou didst march through
        the wilderness,   *Selah*
⁸the earth quaked, the heavens
    poured down rain,
    at the presence of God;
    yon Sinai quaked at the presence of
        God,
    the God of Israel.
⁹Rain in abundance, O God, thou
    didst shed abroad;
    thou didst restore thy heritage as
        it languished;
¹⁰thy flock found a dwelling in it;
    in thy goodness, O God, thou
        didst provide for the needy.

¹¹The Lord gives the command;
    great is the host of those who bore
        the tidings:

¹²"The kings of the armies, they flee,
    they flee!"
    The women at home divide the
        spoil,
¹³   though they stay among the
        sheepfolds—
    the wings of a dove covered with
        silver,
    its pinions with green gold.
¹⁴When the Almighty scattered kings
    there,
    snow fell on Zalmon.
¹⁵O mighty mountain, mountain of
    Bashan;
    O many-peaked mountain,
    mountain of Bashan!
¹⁶Why look you with envy, O many-
    peaked mountain,
    at the mount which God desired
        for his abode,
    yea, where the LORD will dwell
        for ever?
¹⁷With mighty chariotry, twice ten
    thousand,
    thousands upon thousands,
    the Lord came from Sinai into the
        holy place.
¹⁸Thou didst ascend the high mount,
    leading captives in thy train,
    and receiving gifts among men,
    even among the rebellious, that the
        LORD God may dwell there.

¹⁹Blessed be the Lord,
    who daily bears us up;
    God is our salvation.   *Selah*
²⁰Our God is a God of salvation;
    and to GOD, the Lord, belongs es-
        cape from death.

²¹But God will shatter the heads of his
    enemies,
    the hairy crown of him who walks
        in his guilty ways.
²²The Lord said,
    "I will bring them back from
        Bashan,
    I will bring them back from the
        depths of the sea,
²³that you may bathe your feet in
    blood,
    that the tongues of your dogs may
        have their portion from the
        foe."

²⁴Thy solemn processions are seen, O
    God,

the processions of my God, my King, into the sanctuary—
25 the singers in front, the minstrels last,
   between them maidens playing timbrels:
26 "Bless God in the great congregation,
   the LORD, O you who are of Israel's fountain!"
27 There is Benjamin, the least of them, in the lead,
   the princes of Judah in their throng,
   the princes of Zeb'ulun, the princes of Naph'tali.

28 Summon thy might, O God;
   show thy strength, O God, thou who hast wrought for us.
29 Because of thy temple at Jerusalem kings bear gifts to thee.
30 Rebuke the beasts that dwell among the reeds,
   the herd of bulls with the calves of the peoples.
   Trample under foot those who lust after tribute;
   scatter the peoples who delight in war.
31 Let bronze be brought from Egypt;
   let Ethiopia hasten to stretch out her hands to God.

32 Sing to God, O kingdoms of the earth;
   sing praises to the Lord,   *Selah*
33 to him who rides in the heavens, the ancient heavens;
   lo, he sends forth his voice, his mighty voice.
34 Ascribe power to God,
   whose majesty is over Israel,
   and his power is in the skies.
35 Terrible is God in his sanctuary, the God of Israel,
   he gives power and strength to his people.
   Blessed be God!

To the choirmaster: according to Lilies. A Psalm of David.

69 Save me, O God!
For the waters have come up to my neck.

2 I sink in deep mire,
   where there is no foothold;
   I have come into deep waters,
   and the flood sweeps over me.
3 I am weary with my crying;
   my throat is parched.
   My eyes grow dim
   with waiting for my God.
4 More in number than the hairs of my head
   are those who hate me without cause;
   mighty are those who would destroy me,
   those who attack me with lies.
   What I did not steal
   must I now restore?

5 O God, thou knowest my folly;
   the wrongs I have done are not hidden from thee.

6 Let not those who hope in thee be put to shame through me,
   O Lord GOD of hosts;
   let not those who seek thee be brought to dishonor through me,
   O God of Israel.
7 For it is for thy sake that I have borne reproach,
   that shame has covered my face.
8 I have become a stranger to my brethren,
   an alien to my mother's sons.

9 For zeal for thy house has consumed me,
   and the insults of those who insult thee have fallen on me.
10 When I humbled my soul with fasting,
   it became my reproach.
11 When I made sackcloth my clothing,
   I became a byword to them.
12 I am the talk of those who sit in the gate,
   and the drunkards make songs about me.

13 But as for me, my prayer is to thee, O LORD.
   At an acceptable time, O God,
   in the abundance of thy steadfast love answer me.
   With thy faithful help 14 rescue me from sinking in the mire;

let me be delivered from my
enemies
and from the deep waters.
15 Let not the flood sweep over me,
or the deep swallow me up,
or the pit close its mouth over me.
16 Answer me, O LORD, for thy steadfast love is good;
according to thy abundant mercy,
turn to me.
17 Hide not thy face from thy servant;
for I am in distress, make haste to
answer me.
18 Draw near to me, redeem me,
set me free because of my
enemies!
19 Thou knowest my reproach,
and my shame and my dishonor;
my foes are all known to thee.
20 Insults have broken my heart,
so that I am in despair.
I looked for pity, but there was none;
and for comforters, but I found
none.
21 They gave me poison for food,
and for my thirst they gave me
vinegar to drink.

22 Let their own table before them become a snare;
let their sacrificial feasts be a trap.
23 Let their eyes be darkened, so that
they cannot see;
and make their loins tremble continually.
24 Pour out thy indignation upon
them,
and let thy burning anger over-
take them.
25 May their camp be a desolation,
let no one dwell in their tents.
26 For they persecute him whom thou
hast smitten,
and him whom thou hast
wounded, they afflict still more.
27 Add to them punishment upon
punishment;
may they have no acquittal from
thee.
28 Let them be blotted out of the book
of the living;
let them not be enrolled among
the righteous.

29 But I am afflicted and in pain;
let thy salvation, O God, set me
on high!

30 I will praise the name of God with a
song;
I will magnify him with thanksgiving.
31 This will please the LORD more than
an ox
or a bull with horns and hoofs.
32 Let the oppressed see it and be glad;
you who seek God, let your hearts
revive.
33 For the LORD hears the needy,
and does not despise his own that
are in bonds.

34 Let heaven and earth praise him,
the seas and everything that
moves therein.
35 For God will save Zion
and rebuild the cities of Judah;
and his servants shall dwell there
and possess it;
36 the children of his servants shall
inherit it,
and those who love his name shall
dwell in it.

To the choirmaster. A Psalm of David,
for the memorial offering.

70 Be pleased, O God, to deliver
me!
O LORD, make haste to help me!
2 Let them be put to shame and confusion
who seek my life!
Let them be turned back and
brought to dishonor
who desire my hurt!
3 Let them be appalled because of
their shame
who say, "Aha, Aha!"

4 May all who seek thee
rejoice and be glad in thee!
May those who love thy salvation
say evermore, "God is great!"
5 But I am poor and needy;
hasten to me, O God!
Thou art my help and my deliverer;
O LORD, do not tarry!

71 In thee, O LORD, do I take
refuge;
let me never be put to shame!

2 In thy righteousness deliver me and
rescue me;
incline thy ear to me, and save
me!
3 Be thou to me a rock of refuge,
a strong fortress, to save me,
for thou art my rock and my fortress.
4 Rescue me, O my God, from the
hand of the wicked,
from the grasp of the unjust and
cruel man.
5 For thou, O Lord, art my hope,
my trust, O LORD, from my youth.
6 Upon thee I have leaned from my
birth;
thou art he who took me from my
mother's womb.
My praise is continually of thee.

7 I have been as a portent to many;
but thou art my strong refuge.
8 My mouth is filled with thy praise,
and with thy glory all the day.
9 Do not cast me off in the time of old
age;
forsake me not when my strength
is spent.
10 For my enemies speak concerning
me,
those who watch for my life consult together,
11 and say, "God has forsaken him;
pursue and seize him,
for there is none to deliver him."

12 O God, be not far from me;
O my God, make haste to help
me!
13 May my accusers be put to shame
and consumed;
with scorn and disgrace may they
be covered
who seek my hurt.
14 But I will hope continually,
and will praise thee yet more and
more.
15 My mouth will tell of thy righteous
acts,
of thy deeds of salvation all the
day,
for their number is past my
knowledge.
16 With the mighty deeds of the Lord
GOD I will come,
I will praise thy righteousness,
thine alone.

17 O God, from my youth thou hast
taught me,
and I still proclaim thy wondrous
deeds.
18 So even to old age and gray hairs,
O God, do not forsake me,
till I proclaim thy might
to all the generations to come.
Thy power 19 and thy righteousness,
O God,
reach the high heavens.
Thou who hast done great things,
O God, who is like thee?
20 Thou who hast made me see many
sore troubles
wilt revive me again;
from the depths of the earth
thou wilt bring me up again.
21 Thou wilt increase my honor,
and comfort me again.
22 I will also praise thee with the harp
for thy faithfulness, O my God;
I will sing praises to thee with the
lyre,
O Holy One of Israel.
23 My lips will shout for joy,
when I sing praises to thee;
my soul also, which thou hast rescued.
24 And my tongue will talk of thy
righteous help
all the day long,
for they have been put to shame and
disgraced
who sought to do me hurt.

A Psalm of Solomon.

72 Give the king thy justice, O
God,
and thy righteousness to the royal
son!
2 May he judge thy people with righteousness,
and thy poor with justice!
3 Let the mountains bear prosperity
for the people,
and the hills, in righteousness!
4 May he defend the cause of the poor
of the people,
give deliverance to the needy,
and crush the oppressor!

5 May he live while the sun endures,
and as long as the moon,
throughout all generations!

⁶May he be like rain that falls on the mown grass,
like showers that water the earth!
⁷In his days may righteousness flourish,
and peace abound, till the moon be no more!
⁸May he have dominion from sea to sea,
and from the River to the ends of the earth!
⁹May his foes bow down before him,
and his enemies lick the dust!
¹⁰May the kings of Tarshish and of the isles
render him tribute,
may the kings of Sheba and Seba bring gifts!
¹¹May all kings fall down before him,
all nations serve him!

¹²For he delivers the needy when he calls,
the poor and him who has no helper.
¹³He has pity on the weak and the needy,
and saves the lives of the needy.
¹⁴From oppression and violence he redeems their life;
and precious is their blood in his sight.

¹⁵Long may he live,
may gold of Sheba be given to him!
May prayer be made for him continually,
and blessings invoked for him all the day!
¹⁶May there be abundance of grain in the land;
on the tops of the mountains may it wave;
may its fruit be like Lebanon;
and may men blossom forth from the cities
like the grass of the field!
¹⁷May his name endure for ever,
his fame continue as long as the sun!
May men bless themselves by him,
all nations call him blessed!

¹⁸Blessed be the LORD, the God of Israel,
who alone does wondrous things.

¹⁹Blessed be his glorious name for ever;
may his glory fill the whole earth!
Amen and Amen!
²⁰The prayers of David, the son of Jesse, are ended.

BOOK III

A Psalm of Asaph.

73 Truly God is good to the upright,
to those who are pure in heart.
²But as for me, my feet had almost stumbled,
my steps had well nigh slipped.
³For I was envious of the arrogant,
when I saw the prosperity of the wicked.

⁴For they have no pangs;
their bodies are sound and sleek.
⁵They are not in trouble as other men are;
they are not stricken like other men.
⁶Therefore pride is their necklace;
violence covers them as a garment.
⁷Their eyes swell out with fatness,
their hearts overflow with follies.
⁸They scoff and speak with malice;
loftily they threaten oppression.
⁹They set their mouths against the heavens,
and their tongue struts through the earth.
¹⁰Therefore the people turn and praise them;
and find no fault in them.
¹¹And they say, "How can God know?
Is there knowledge in the Most High?"
¹²Behold, these are the wicked;
always at ease, they increase in riches.
¹³All in vain have I kept my heart clean
and washed my hands in innocence.
¹⁴For all the day long I have been stricken,
and chastened every morning.

15 If I had said, "I will speak thus,"
   I would have been untrue to the
      generation of thy children.
16 But when I thought how to under-
      stand this,
   it seemed to me a wearisome task,
17 until I went into the sanctuary of
      God;
   then I perceived their end.
18 Truly thou dost set them in slippery
      places;
   thou dost make them fall to ruin.
19 How they are destroyed in a mo-
      ment,
   swept away utterly by terrors!
20 They are like a dream when one
      awakes,
   on awaking you despise their
      phantoms.

21 When my soul was embittered,
   when I was pricked in heart,
22 I was stupid and ignorant,
   I was like a beast toward thee.
23 Nevertheless I am continually with
      thee;
   thou dost hold my right hand.
24 Thou dost guide me with thy coun-
      sel,
   and afterward thou wilt receive
      me to glory.
25 Whom have I in heaven but thee?
   And there is nothing upon earth
      that I desire besides thee.
26 My flesh and my heart may fail,
   but God is the strength of my
      heart and my portion for ever.

27 For lo, those who are far from thee
      shall perish;
   thou dost put an end to those who
      are false to thee.
28 But for me it is good to be near God;
   I have made the Lord GOD my ref-
      uge,
   that I may tell of all thy works.

A Maskil of Asaph.

74

O God, why dost thou cast us
off for ever?
   Why does thy anger smoke
      against the sheep of thy
      pasture?
2 Remember thy congregation, which
   thou hast gotten of old,
which thou hast redeemed to be
   the tribe of thy heritage!
Remember Mount Zion, where
   thou hast dwelt.
3 Direct thy steps to the perpetual
   ruins;
   the enemy has destroyed every-
      thing in the sanctuary!

4 Thy foes have roared in the midst of
   thy holy place;
   they set up their own signs for
      signs.
5 At the upper entrance they hacked
   the wooden trellis with axes.
6 And then all its carved wood
   they broke down with hatchets
      and hammers.
7 They set thy sanctuary on fire;
   to the ground they desecrated the
      dwelling place of thy name.
8 They said to themselves, "We will
   utterly subdue them";
   they burned all the meeting places
      of God in the land.

9 We do not see our signs;
   there is no longer any prophet,
   and there is none among us who
      knows how long.
10 How long, O God, is the foe to scoff?
   Is the enemy to revile thy name
      for ever?
11 Why dost thou hold back thy hand,
   why dost thou keep thy right
      hand in thy bosom?

12 Yet God my King is from of old,
   working salvation in the midst of
      the earth.

13 Thou didst divide the sea by thy
      might;
   thou didst break the heads of the
      dragons on the waters.
14 Thou didst crush the heads of
      Leviathan,
   thou didst give him as food for the
      creatures of the wilderness.
15 Thou didst cleave open springs and
      brooks;
   thou didst dry up ever-flowing
      streams.
16 Thine is the day, thine also the
      night;
   thou hast established the lumin-
      aries and the sun.

17 Thou hast fixed all the bounds of the earth;
   thou hast made summer and winter.

18 Remember this, O LORD, how the enemy scoffs,
   and an impious people reviles thy name.
19 Do not deliver the soul of thy dove to the wild beasts;
   do not forget the life of thy poor for ever.
20 Have regard for thy covenant;
   for the dark places of the land are full of the habitations of violence.
21 Let not the downtrodden be put to shame;
   let the poor and needy praise thy name.

22 Arise, O God, plead thy cause;
   remember how the impious scoff at thee all the day!
23 Do not forget the clamor of thy foes,
   the uproar of thy adversaries which goes up continually!

To the choirmaster: according to Do Not Destroy. A Psalm of Asaph. A Song.

75 We give thanks to thee, O God; we give thanks;
   we call on thy name and recount thy wondrous deeds.

2 At the set time which I appoint
   I will judge with equity.
3 When the earth totters, and all its inhabitants,
   it is I who keep steady its pillars. *Selah*
4 I say to the boastful, "Do not boast,"
   and to the wicked, "Do not lift up your horn;
5 do not lift up your horn on high,
   or speak with insolent neck."

6 For not from the east or from the west
   and not from the wilderness comes lifting up;
7 but it is God who executes judgment,

putting down one and lifting up another.
8 For in the hand of the LORD there is a cup,
   with foaming wine, well mixed;
   and he will pour a draught from it,
   and all the wicked of the earth shall drain it down to the dregs.

9 But I will rejoice for ever,
   I will sing praises to the God of Jacob.
10 All the horns of the wicked he will cut off,
   but the horns of the righteous shall be exalted.

To the choirmaster: with stringed instruments. A Psalm of Asaph. A Song.

76 In Judah God is known,
   his name is great in Israel.
2 His abode has been established in Salem,
   his dwelling place in Zion.
3 There he broke the flashing arrows,
   the shield, the sword, and the weapons of war. *Selah*

4 Glorious art thou, more majestic
   than the everlasting mountains.
5 The stouthearted were stripped of their spoil;
   they sank into sleep;
   all the men of war
   were unable to use their hands.
6 At thy rebuke, O God of Jacob,
   both rider and horse lay stunned.

7 But thou, terrible art thou!
   Who can stand before thee
   when once thy anger is roused?
8 From the heavens thou didst utter judgment;
   the earth feared and was still,
9 when God arose to establish judgment
   to save all the oppressed of the earth. *Selah*

10 Surely the wrath of men shall praise thee;
   the residue of wrath thou wilt gird upon thee.
11 Make your vows to the LORD your God, and perform them;

let all around him bring gifts
to him who is to be feared,
¹²who cuts off the spirit of princes,
who is terrible to the kings of the
earth.

To the choirmaster: according to
Jeduthun. A Pslam of Asaph.

77 I cry aloud to God,
aloud to God, that he may hear
me.
²In the day of my trouble I seek the
Lord;
in the night my hand is stretched
out without wearying;
my soul refuses to be comforted.

³I think of God, and I moan;
I meditate, and my spirit faints.
Selah
⁴Thou dost hold my eyelids from
closing;
I am so troubled that I cannot
speak.
⁵I consider the days of old,
I remember the years long ago.
⁶I commune with my heart in the
night;
I meditate and search my spirit:
⁷"Will the Lord spurn for ever,
and never again be favorable?
⁸Has his steadfast love for ever
ceased?
Are his promises at an end for all
time?
⁹Has God forgotten to be gracious?
Has he in anger shut up his compassion?" *Selah*
¹⁰And I say, "It is my grief
that the right hand of the Most
High has changed."

¹¹I will call to mind the deeds of the
LORD;
yea, I will remember thy wonders
of old.
¹²I will meditate on all thy work,
and muse on thy mighty deeds.

¹³Thy way, O God, is holy.
What god is great like our God?
¹⁴Thou art the God who workest
wonders,
who hast manifested thy might
among the peoples.

¹⁵Thou didst with thy arm redeem thy
people,
the sons of Jacob and Joseph.
Selah
¹⁶When the waters saw thee, O God,
when the waters saw thee, they
were afraid,
yea, the deep trembled.
¹⁷The clouds poured out water;
the skies gave forth thunder;
thy arrows flashed on every side.
¹⁸The crash of thy thunder was in the
whirlwind;
thy lightnings lighted up the
world;
the earth trembled and shook.
¹⁹Thy way was through the sea,
thy path through the great waters;
yet thy footprints were unseen.
²⁰Thou didst lead thy people like a
flock
by the hand of Moses and Aaron.

A Maskil of Asaph.

78 Give ear, O my people, to my
teaching;
incline your ears to the words of
my mouth!
²I will open my mouth in a parable;
I will utter dark sayings from of
old,
³things that we have heard and
known,
that our fathers have told us.
⁴We will not hide them from their
children,
but tell to the coming generation
the glorious deeds of the LORD, and
his might,
and the wonders which he has
wrought.

⁵He established a testimony in Jacob,
and appointed a law in Israel,
which he commanded our fathers
to teach to their children;
⁶that the next generation might know
them,
the children yet unborn,
and arise and tell them to their children,
⁷ so that they should set their hope
in God,
and not forget the works of God,
but keep his commandments;

⁸and that they should not be like their fathers,
a stubborn and rebellious generation,
a generation whose heart was not steadfast,
whose spirit was not faithful to God.

⁹The E'phraimites, armed with the bow,
turned back on the day of battle.
¹⁰They did not keep God's covenant,
but refused to walk according to his law.
¹¹They forgot what he had done,
and the miracles that he had shown them.
¹²In the sight of their fathers he wrought marvels
in the land of Egypt, in the fields of Zo'an.
¹³He divided the sea and let them pass through it,
and made the waters stand like a heap.
¹⁴In the daytime he had led them with a cloud,
and all the night with a fiery light.
¹⁵He cleft rocks in the wilderness,
and gave them drink abundantly as from the deep.
¹⁶He made streams come out of the rock,
and caused waters to flow down like rivers.

¹⁷Yet they sinned still more against him,
rebelling against the Most High in the desert.
¹⁸They tested God in their heart
by demanding the food they craved.
¹⁹They spoke against God, saying,
"Can God spread a table in the wilderness?
²⁰He smote the rock so that water gushed out
and streams overflowed.
Can he also give bread,
or provide meat for his people?"

²¹Therefore, when the LORD heard,
he was full of wrath;
a fire was kindled against Jacob,
his anger mounted against Israel;
²²because they had no faith in God,
and did not trust his saving power.
²³Yet he commanded the skies above,
and opened the doors of heaven;
²⁴and he rained down upon them manna to eat,
and gave them the grain of heaven.
²⁵Man ate of the bread of the angels;
he sent them food in abundance.
²⁶He caused the east wind to blow in the heavens,
and by his power he led out the south wind;
²⁷he rained flesh upon them like dust,
winged birds like the sand of the seas;
²⁸he let them fall in the midst of their camp,
all around their habitations.
²⁹And they ate and were well filled,
for he gave them what they craved.
³⁰But before they had sated their craving,
while the food was still in their mouths,
³¹the anger of God rose against them
and he slew the strongest of them,
and laid low the picked men of Israel.

³²In spite of all this they still sinned;
despite his wonders they did not believe.
³³So he made their days vanish like a breath,
and their years in terror.
³⁴When he slew them, they sought for him;
they repented and sought God earnestly.
³⁵They remembered that God was their rock,
the Most High God their redeemer.
³⁶But they flattered him with their mouths;
they lied to him with their tongues.
³⁷Their heart was not steadfast toward him;
they were not true to his covenant.
³⁸Yet he, being compassionate,
forgave their iniquity,

and did not destroy them;
he restrained his anger often,
and did not stir up all his wrath.
[39] He remembered that they were but flesh,
a wind that passes and comes not again.

[40] How often they rebelled against him in the wilderness
and grieved him in the desert!
[41] They tested him again and again,
and provoked the Holy One of Israel.
[42] They did not keep in mind his power,
or the day when he redeemed them from the foe;
[43] when he wrought his signs in Egypt,
and his miracles in the fields of Zo'an.
[44] He turned their rivers to blood,
so that they could not drink of their streams.
[45] He sent among them swarms of flies, which devoured them,
and frogs, which destroyed them.
[46] He gave their crops to the caterpillar,
and the fruit of their labor to the locust.
[47] He destroyed their vines with hail,
and their sycamores with frost.
[48] He gave over their cattle to the hail,
and their flocks to thunderbolts.
[49] He let loose on them his fierce anger,
wrath, indignation, and distress,
a company of destroying angels.
[50] He made a path for his anger;
he did not spare them from death,
but gave their lives over to the plague.
[51] He smote all the first-born in Egypt,
the first issue of their strength in the tents of Ham.
[52] Then he led forth his people like sheep,
and guided them in the wilderness like a flock.
[53] He led them in safety, so that they were not afraid;
but the sea overwhelmed their enemies.
[54] And he brought them to his holy land,
to the mountain which his right hand had won.

[55] He drove out nations before them;
he apportioned them for a possession
and settled the tribes of Israel in their tents.

[56] Yet they tested and rebelled against the Most High God,
and did not observe his testimonies,
[57] but turned away and acted treacherously like their fathers;
they twisted like a deceitful bow.
[58] For they provoked him to anger with their high places;
they moved him to jealousy with their graven images.
[59] When God heard, he was full of wrath,
and he utterly rejected Israel.
[60] He forsook his dwelling at Shiloh,
the tent where he dwelt among men,
[61] and delivered his power to captivity,
his glory to the hand of the foe.
[62] He gave his people over to the sword,
and vented his wrath on his heritage.
[63] Fire devoured their young men,
and their maidens had no marriage song.
[64] Their priests fell by the sword,
and their widows made no lamentation.
[65] Then the Lord awoke as from sleep,
like a strong man shouting because of wine.
[66] And he put his adversaries to rout;
he put them to everlasting shame.

[67] He rejected the tent of Joseph,
he did not choose the tribe of E'phraim;
[68] but he chose the tribe of Judah,
Mount Zion, which he loves.
[69] He built his sanctuary like the high heavens,
like the earth, which he has founded for ever.
[70] He chose David his servant,
and took him from the sheepfolds;
[71] from tending the ewes that had young he brought him
to be the shepherd of Jacob his people,
of Israel his inheritance.

⁷²With upright heart he tended them,
    and guided them with skilful
    hand.

A Psalm of Asaph.

79 O God, the heathen have come
    into thy inheritance;
they have defiled thy holy temple;
they have laid Jerusalem in ruins.
²They have given the bodies of thy
    servants
    to the birds of the air for food,
    the flesh of thy saints to the beasts
    of the earth.
³They have poured out their blood
    like water
    round about Jerusalem,
    and there was none to bury them.
⁴We have become a taunt to our
    neighbors,
    mocked and derided by those
    round about us.

⁵How long, O LORD? Wilt thou be
    angry for ever?
Will thy jealous wrath burn like
    fire?
⁶Pour out thy anger on the nations
    that do not know thee,
    and on the kingdoms
    that do not call on thy name!
⁷For they have devoured Jacob,
    and laid waste his habitation.

⁸Do not remember against us the in-
    iquities of our forefathers;
    let thy compassion come speedily
    to meet us,
    for we are brought very low.

⁹Help us, O God of our salvation,
    for the glory of thy name;
    deliver us, and forgive our sins,
    for thy name's sake!
¹⁰Why should the nations say,
    "Where is their God?"
Let the avenging of the outpoured
    blood of thy servants
    be known among the nations be-
    fore our eyes!

¹¹Let the groans of the prisoners come
    before thee;
    according to thy great power pre-
    serve those doomed to die!

¹²Return sevenfold into the bosom of
    our neighbors
    the taunts with which they have
    taunted thee, O Lord!
¹³Then we thy people, the flock of thy
    pasture,
    will give thanks to thee for ever;
    from generation to generation we
    will recount thy praise.

To the choirmaster: according to Lilies.
A Testimony of Asaph. A Psalm.

80 Give ear, O Shepherd of Israel,
    thou who leadest Joseph like a
    flock!
Thou who are enthroned upon the
    cherubim, shine forth
²   before E'phraim and Benjamin
    and Manas'seh!
Stir up thy might,
    and come to save us!

³Restore us, O God;
    let thy face shine, that we may be
    saved!

⁴O LORD God of hosts,
    how long wilt thou be angry with
    thy people's prayers?
⁵Thou hast fed them with the bread
    of tears,
    and given them tears to drink in
    full measure.
⁶Thou dost make us the scorn of our
    neighbors;
    and our enemies laugh among
    themselves.

⁷Restore us, O God of hosts;
    let thy face shine, that we may be
    saved!

⁸Thou didst bring a vine out of
    Egypt;
    thou didst drive out the nations
    and plant it.
⁹Thou didst clear the ground for it;
    it took deep root and filled the
    land.
¹⁰The mountains were covered with
    its shade,
    the mighty cedars with its
    branches;
¹¹it sent out its branches to the sea,
    and its shoots to the River.

12 Why then hast thou broken down its
walls,
so that all who pass along the way
pluck its fruit?
13 The boar from the forest ravages it,
and all that move in the field feed
on it.

14 Turn again, O God of hosts!
Look down from heaven, and see;
have regard for this vine,
15 the stock which thy right hand
planted.
16 They have burned it with fire, they
have cut it down;
may they perish at the rebuke of
thy countenance!
17 But let thy hand be upon the man of
thy right hand,
the son of man whom thou hast
made strong for thyself!
18 Then we will never turn back from
thee;
give us life, and we will call on thy
name!
19 Restore us, O LORD God of hosts!
let thy face shine, that we may be
saved!

To the choirmaster: according to The
Gittith. A Psalm of Asaph.

81 Sing aloud to God our strength;
shout for joy to the God of Jacob!
2 Raise a song, sound the timbrel,
the sweet lyre with the harp.
3 Blow the trumpet at the new moon,
at the full moon, on our feast day.
4 For it is a statute for Israel,
an ordinance of the God of
Jacob.
5 He made it a decree in Joseph,
when he went out over the land of
Egypt.

I hear a voice I had not known:
6 "I relieved your shoulder of the burden;
your hands were freed from the
basket.
7 In distress you called, and I delivered you;
I answered you in the secret place
of thunder;
I tested you at the waters of
Mer'ibah.   *Selah*

8 Hear, O my people, while I ad-
monish you!
O Israel, if you would but listen to
me!
9 There shall be no strange god among
you;
you shall not bow down to a
foreign god.
10 I am the LORD your God,
who brought you up out of the
land of Egypt.
Open your mouth wide, and I will
fill it.

11 "But my people did not listen to my
voice;
Israel would have none of me.
12 So I gave them over to their stubborn hearts,
to follow their own counsels.
13 O that my people would listen to
me,
that Israel would walk in my
ways!
14 I would soon subdue their enemies,
and turn my hand against their
foes.
15 Those who hate the LORD would
cringe toward him,
and their fate would last for ever.
16 I would feed you with the finest of
the wheat,
and with honey from the rock I
would satisfy you."

A Psalm of Asaph.

82 God has taken his place in the
divine council;
in the midst of the gods he holds
judgment:
2 "How long will you judge unjustly
and show partiality to the wicked?
Selah
3 Give justice to the weak and the
fatherless;
maintain the right of the afflicted
and the destitute.
4 Rescue the weak and the needy;
deliver them from the hand of the
wicked."
5 They have neither knowledge nor
understanding,
they walk about in darkness;
all the foundations of the earth are
shaken.

⁶I say, "You are gods,
sons of the Most High, all of you;
⁷nevertheless, you shall die like men,
and fall like any prince."

⁸Arise, O God, judge the earth;
for to thee belong all the nations!

A Song. A Psalm of Asaph.

83 O God, do not keep silence;
do not hold thy peace or be still,
O God!
²For lo, thy enemies are in tumult;
those who hate thee have raised
their heads.
³They lay crafty plans against thy
people;
they consult together against thy
protected ones.
⁴They say, "Come, let us wipe them
out as a nation;
let the name of Israel be remembered no more!"
⁵Yea, they conspire with one accord;
against thee they make a covenant—
⁶the tents of Edom and the Ish'mae-
lites,
Moab and the Hagrites,
⁷Gebal and Ammon and Am'alek,
Philistia with the inhabitants of
Tyre;
⁸Assyria also has joined them;
they are the strong arm of the
children of Lot.   *Selah*

⁹Do to them as thou didst to Mid'ian,
as to Sis'era and Jabin at the river
Kishon,
¹⁰who were destroyed at En-dor,
who became dung for the ground.
¹¹Make their nobles like Oreb and
Zeeb,
all their princes like Zebah and
Zalmun'na,
¹²who said, "Let us take possession
for ourselves
of the pastures of God."

¹³O my God, make them like whirling
dust,
like chaff before the wind.
¹⁴As fire consumes the forest,
as the flame sets the mountains
ablaze,

¹⁵so do thou pursue them with thy
tempest
and terrify them with thy hur-
ricane!
¹⁶Fill their faces with shame,
that they may seek thy name, O
LORD.
¹⁷Let them be put to shame and dismayed for ever;
let them perish in disgrace.
¹⁸Let them know that thou alone,
whose name is the LORD,
art the Most High over all the
earth.

To the choirmaster: according to The
Gittith. A Psalm of the Sons of Korah.

84 How lovely is thy dwelling
place,
O LORD of hosts!
²My soul longs, yea, faints
for the courts of the LORD;
my heart and flesh sing for joy to the
living God.

³Even the sparrow finds a home,
and the swallow a nest for herself,
where she may lay her young,
at thy altars, O LORD of hosts,
my King and my God.
⁴Blessed are those who dwell in thy
house,
ever singing thy praise!   *Selah*

⁵Blessed are the men whose strength
is in thee,
in whose heart are the highways
to Zion.
⁶As they go through the valley of
Baca
they make it a place of springs;
the early rain also covers it with
pools.
⁷They go from strength to strength;
the God of gods will be seen in
Zion.

⁸O LORD God of hosts, hear my
prayer;
give ear, O God of Jacob!   *Selah*
⁹Behold our shield, O God;
look upon the face of thine
anointed!
¹⁰For a day in thy courts is better
than a thousand elsewhere.

I would rather be a doorkeeper in
    the house of my God
  than dwell in the tents of wicked-
    ness.
[11]For the LORD God is a sun and
    shield;
  he bestows favor and honor.
No good thing does the LORD with-
    hold
  from those who walk uprightly.
[12]O LORD of hosts,
  blessed is the man who trusts in
    thee!

To the choirmaster. A Psalm of the
Sons of Korah.

85 LORD, thou wast favorable to
thy land;
  thou didst restore the fortunes of
    Jacob.
[2]Thou didst forgive the iniquity of
    thy people;
  thou didst pardon all their sin.
                  Selah
[3]Thou didst withdraw all thy wrath;
  thou didst turn from thy hot
    anger.

[4]Restore us again, O God of our sal-
    vation,
  and put away thy indignation
    toward us!
[5]Wilt thou be angry with us for ever?
  Wilt thou prolong thy anger to all
    generations?
[6]Wilt thou not revive us again,
  that thy people may rejoice in
    thee?
[7]Show us thy steadfast love, O LORD,
  and grant us thy salvation.

[8]Let me hear what God the LORD will
    speak,
  for he will speak peace to his
    people,
  to his saints, to those who turn to
    him in their hearts.
[9]Surely his salvation is at hand for
    those who fear him,
  that glory may dwell in our land.

[10]Steadfast love and faithfulness will
    meet;
  righteousness and peace will kiss
    each other.

[11]Faithfulness will spring up from the
    ground,
  and righteousness will look down
    from the sky.
[12]Yea, the LORD will give what is
    good,
  and our land will yield its in-
    crease.
[13]Righteousness will go before him,
  and make his footsteps a way.

A Prayer of David.

86 Incline thy ear, O LORD, and
answer me,
  for I am poor and needy.
[2]Preserve my life, for I am godly;
  save thy servant who trusts in
    thee.
Thou art my God; [3] be gracious to
    me, O Lord,
  for to thee do I cry all the day.
[4]Gladden the soul of thy servant,
  for to thee, O Lord, do I lift up my
    soul.
[5]For thou, O Lord, art good and for-
    giving,
  abounding in steadfast love to all
    who call on thee.
[6]Give ear, O LORD, to my prayer;
  hearken to my cry of supplication.
[7]In the day of my trouble I call on
    thee,
  for thou dost answer me.
[8]There is none like thee among the
    gods, O Lord,
  nor are there any works like thine.
[9]All the nations thou hast made shall
    come
  and bow down before thee, O
    Lord,
  and shall glorify thy name.
[10]For thou art great and doest won-
    drous things,
  thou alone art God.
[11]Teach me thy way, O LORD,
  that I may walk in thy truth;
  unite my heart to fear thy name.
[12]I give thanks to thee, O Lord my
    God, with my whole heart,
  and I will glorify thy name for
    ever.
[13]For great is thy steadfast love toward
    me;
  thou hast delivered my soul from
    the depths of Sheol.

14 O God, insolent men have risen up
   against me;
a band of ruthless men seek my
   life,
and they do not set thee before
   them.
15 But thou, O Lord, art a God merciful
   and gracious,
   slow to anger and abounding in
   steadfast love and faithfulness.
16 Turn to me and take pity on me;
   give thy strength to thy servant,
   and save the son of thy handmaid.
17 Show me a sign of thy favor,
   that those who hate me may see
   and be put to shame
   because thou, LORD, hast helped
   me and comforted me.

A Psalm of the Sons of Korah. A Song.

87 On the holy mount stands the
city he founded;
2   the LORD loves the gates of Zion
   more than all the dwelling places
   of Jacob.
3 Glorious things are spoken of you,
   O city of God.   *Selah*

4 Among those who know me I mention Rahab and Babylon;
   behold, Philistia and Tyre, with
   Ethiopia—
   "This one was born there," they
   say.
5 And of Zion it shall be said,
   "This one and that one were born
   in her";
   for the Most High himself will establish her.
6 The LORD records as he registers the
   peoples,
   "This one was born there." *Selah*

7 Singers and dancers alike say,
   "All my springs are in you."

A Song. A Psalm of the Sons of Korah.
To the choirmaster: according to
   Mahalath Leannoth. A Maskil of
   Heman the Ezrahite.

88 O LORD, my God, I call for
help by day;
   I cry out in the night before thee.

2 Let my prayer come before thee,
   incline thy ear to my cry!

3 For my soul is full of troubles,
   and my life draws near to Sheol.
4 I am reckoned among those who go
   down to the Pit;
   I am a man who has no strength,
5 like one forsaken among the dead,
   like the slain that lie in the grave,
   like those whom thou dost remember no more,
   for they are cut off from thy hand.
6 Thou hast put me in the depths of
   the Pit,
   in the regions dark and deep.
7 Thy wrath lies heavy upon me,
   and thou dost overwhelm me with
   all thy waves.   *Selah*
8 Thou hast caused my companions to
   shun me;
   thou hast made me a thing of horror to them.
   I am shut in so that I cannot escape;
9   my eye grows dim through sorrow.
   Every day I call upon thee, O LORD;
   I spread out my hands to thee.
10 Dost thou work wonders for the
   dead?
   Do the shades rise up to praise
   thee?   *Selah*
11 Is thy steadfast love declared in the
   grave,
   or thy faithfulness in Abaddon?
12 Are thy wonders known in the
   darkness,
   or thy saving help in the land of
   forgetfulness?

13 But I, O LORD, cry to thee;
   in the morning my prayer comes
   before thee.
14 O LORD, why dost thou cast me off?
   Why dost thou hide thy face from
   me?
15 Afflicted and close to death from my
   youth up,
   I suffer thy terrors; I am helpless.
16 Thy wrath has swept over me;
   thy dread assaults destroy me.
17 They surround me like a flood all
   day long;
   they close in upon me together.
18 Thou hast caused lover and friend to
   shun me;
   my companions are in darkness.

A Maskil of Ethan the Ezrahite.

89 I will sing of thy steadfast love,
O LORD, for ever;
with my mouth I will proclaim thy
faithfulness to all generations.
2 For thy steadfast love was established for ever,
thy faithfulness is firm as the
heavens.
3 Thou hast said, "I have made a covenant with my chosen one,
I have sworn to David my servant:
4 'I will establish your descendants for
ever,
and build your throne for all generations.' " *Selah*

5 Let the heavens praise thy wonders,
O LORD,
thy faithfulness in the assembly of
the holy ones!
6 For who in the skies can be com-
pared to the LORD?
Who among the heavenly beings
is like the LORD,
7 a God feared in the council of the
holy ones,
great and terrible above all that
are round about him?
8 O LORD God of hosts,
who is mighty as thou art, O
LORD,
with thy faithfulness round about
thee?
9 Thou dost rule the raging of the sea;
when its waves rise, thou stillest
them.
10 Thou didst crush Rahab like a car-
cass,
thou didst scatter thy enemies
with thy mighty arm.
11 The heavens are thine, the earth also
is thine;
the world and all that is in it,
thou hast founded them.
12 The north and the south, thou hast
created them;
Tabor and Hermon joyously
praise thy name.
13 Thou hast a mighty arm;
strong is thy hand, high thy right
hand.
14 Righteousness and justice are the
foundation of thy throne;
steadfast love and faithfulness go
before thee.

15 Blessed are the people who know
the festal shout,
who walk, O LORD, in the light of
thy countenance,
16 who exult in thy name all the day,
and extol thy righteousness.
17 For thou art the glory of their
strength;
by thy favor our horn is exalted.
18 For our shield belongs to the LORD,
our king to the Holy One of Israel.

19 Of old thou didst speak in a vision
to thy faithful one, and say:
"I have set the crown upon one who
is mighty,
I have exalted one chosen from the
people.
20 I have found David, my servant;
with my holy oil I have anointed
him;
21 so that my hand shall ever abide
with him,
my arm also shall strengthen him.
22 The enemy shall not outwit him,
the wicked shall not humble him.
23 I will crush his foes before him
and strike down those who hate
him.
24 My faithfulness and my steadfast
love shall be with him,
and in my name shall his horn be
exalted.
25 I will set his hand on the sea
and his right hand on the rivers.

26 "He shall cry to me, 'Thou art my
Father,
my God, and the Rock of my salvation.'
27 And I will make him the first-born,
the highest of the kings of the
earth.
28 My steadfast love I will keep for him
for ever,
and my covenant will stand firm
for him.
29 I will establish his line for ever
and his throne as the days of the
heavens.

30 "If his children forsake my law
and do not walk according to my
ordinances,
31 if they violate my statutes
and do not keep my commandments,

³²then I will punish their transgression with the rod
and their iniquity with scourges;
³³but I will not remove from him my steadfast love,
or be false to my faithfulness.
³⁴I will not violate my covenant,
or alter the word that went forth from my lips.
³⁵Once for all I have sworn by my holiness;
I will not lie to David.
³⁶His line shall endure for ever,
his throne as long as the sun before me.
³⁷Like the moon it shall be established for ever;
it shall stand firm while the skies endure." *Selah*

³⁸But now thou hast cast off and rejected,
thou art full of wrath against thy anointed.
³⁹Thou hast renounced the covenant with thy servant;
thou hast defiled his crown in the dust.
⁴⁰Thou hast breached all his walls;
thou hast laid his strongholds in ruins.
⁴¹All that pass by despoil him;
he has become the scorn of his neighbors.

⁴²Thou hast exalted the right hand of his foes;
thou hast made all his enemies rejoice.
⁴³Yea, thou hast turned back the edge of his sword,
and thou hast not made him stand in battle.
⁴⁴Thou hast removed the scepter from his hand,
and cast his throne to the ground.
⁴⁵Thou hast cut short the days of his youth;
thou hast covered him with shame. *Selah*

⁴⁶How long, O LORD? Wilt thou hide thyself for ever?
How long will thy wrath burn like fire?
⁴⁷Remember, O Lord, what the measure of life is,
for what vanity thou hast created all the sons of men!
⁴⁸What man can live and never see death?
Who can deliver his soul from the power of Sheol? *Selah*
⁴⁹Lord, where is thy steadfast love of old,
which by thy faithfulness thou didst swear to David?
⁵⁰Remember, O Lord, how thy servant is scorned;
how I bear in my bosom the insults of the peoples,
⁵¹with which thy enemies taunt, O LORD,
with which they mock the footsteps of thy anointed.

⁵² Blessed be the LORD for ever!
Amen and Amen.

BOOK IV

A Prayer of Moses, the man of God.

90 Lord, thou hast been our dwelling place
in all generations.
²Before the mountains were brought forth,
or ever thou hadst formed the earth and the world,
from everlasting to everlasting thou art God.
³Thou turnest man back to the dust,
and sayest, "Turn back, O children of men!"
⁴For a thousand years in thy sight
are but as yesterday when it is past,
or as a watch in the night.

⁵Thou dost sweep men away; they are like a dream,
like grass which is renewed in the morning:
⁶in the morning it flourishes and is renewed;
in the evening it fades and withers.
⁷For we are consumed by thy anger;
by thy wrath we are overwhelmed.

⁸Thou hast set our iniquities before
thee,
our secret sins in the light of thy
countenance.

⁹For all our days pass away under thy
wrath,
our years come to an end like a
sigh.
¹⁰The years of our life are threescore
and ten,
or even by reason of strength
fourscore;
yet their span is but toil and trouble;
they are soon gone, and we fly
away.

¹¹Who considers the power of thy
anger,
and thy wrath according to the
fear of thee?
¹²So teach us to number our days
that we may get a heart of wisdom.

¹³Return, O LORD! How long?
Have pity on thy servants!
¹⁴Satisfy us in the morning with thy
steadfast love,
that we may rejoice and be glad all
our days.
¹⁵Make us glad as many days as thou
hast afflicted us,
and as many years as we have
seen evil.
¹⁶Let thy work be manifest to thy servants,
and thy glorious power to their
children.
¹⁷Let the favor of the Lord our God be
upon us,
and establish thou the work of our
hands upon us,
yea, the work of our hands establish thou it.

91 He who dwells in the shelter of
the Most High,
who abides in the shadow of the
Almighty,
²will say to the LORD, "My refuge
and my fortress;
my God, in whom I trust."
³For he will deliver you from the
snare of the fowler
and from the deadly pestilence;

⁴he will cover you with his pinions,
and under his wings you will find
refuge;
his faithfulness is a shield and
buckler.
⁵You will not fear the terror of the
night,
nor the arrow that flies by day,
⁶nor the pestilence that stalks in
darkness,
nor the destruction that wastes at
noonday.
⁷A thousand may fall at your side,
ten thousand at your right hand;
but it will not come near you.
⁸You will only look with your eyes
and see the recompense of the
wicked.

⁹Because you have made the LORD
your refuge,
the Most High your habitation,
¹⁰no evil shall befall you,
no scourge come near your tent.
¹¹For he will give his angels charge of
you
to guard you in all your ways.
¹²On their hands they will bear you
up,
lest you dash your foot against a
stone.
¹³You will tread on the lion and the
adder,
the young lion and the serpent
you will trample under foot.

¹⁴Because he cleaves to me in love, I
will deliver him;
I will protect him, because he
knows my name.
¹⁵When he calls to me, I will answer
him;
I will be with him in trouble,
I will rescue him and honor him.
¹⁶With long life I will satisfy him,
and show him my salvation.

A Psalm. A Song for the Sabbath.

92 It is good to give thanks to the
LORD,
to sing praises to thy name, O
Most High;
²to declare thy steadfast love in the
morning,
and thy faithfulness by night,

3 to the music of the lute and the harp,
  to the melody of the lyre.
4 For thou, O LORD, hast made me
  glad by thy work;
    at the works of thy hands I sing
    for joy.

5 How great are thy works, O LORD!
  Thy thoughts are very deep!
6 The dull man cannot know,
  the stupid cannot understand
  this:
7 that, though the wicked sprout like
  grass
  and all evildoers flourish,
they are doomed to destruction for
  ever,
8   but thou, O LORD, art on high for
    ever.
9 For, lo, thy enemies, O LORD,
  for, lo, thy enemies shall perish;
  all evildoers shall be scattered.

10 But thou hast exalted my horn like
   that of the wild ox;
   thou hast poured over me fresh
   oil.
11 My eyes have seen the downfall of
   my enemies,
   my ears have heard the doom of
   my evil assailants.

12 The righteous flourish like the palm
   tree,
   and grow like a cedar in Lebanon.
13 They are planted in the house of the
   LORD,
   they flourish in the courts of our
   God.
14 They still bring forth fruit in old age,
   they are ever full of sap and green,
15 to show that the LORD is upright;
   he is my rock, and there is no un-
   righteousness in him.

93 The LORD reigns; he is robed in
   majesty;
   the LORD is robed, he is girded
   with strength.
   Yea, the world is established; it shall
   never be moved;
2   thy throne is established from of
    old;
    thou art from everlasting.
3 The floods have lifted up, O LORD,

the floods have lifted up their
  voice,
the floods lift up their roaring.
4 Mightier than the thunders of many
  waters,
  mightier than the waves of the
  sea,
  the LORD, on high is mighty!
5 Thy decrees are very sure;
  holiness befits thy house,
  O LORD, for evermore.

94 O LORD, thou God of vengeance,
   thou God of vengeance, shine
   forth!
2 Rise up, O judge of the earth;
  render to the proud their deserts!
3 O LORD, how long shall the wicked,
  how long shall the wicked exult?
4 They pour out their arrogant words,
  they boast, all the evildoers.
5 They crush thy people, O LORD,
  and afflict thy heritage.
6 They slay the widow and the
  sojourner,
  and murder the fatherless;
7 and they say, "The LORD does not
  see;
  the God of Jacob does not per-
  ceive."

8 Understand, O dullest of the people!
  Fools, when will you be wise?
9 He who planted the ear, does he not
  hear?
  He who formed the eye, does he not
  see?
10 He who chastens the nations, does
   he not chastise?
   He who teaches men knowledge,
11   the LORD, knows the thoughts of
     man,
     that they are but a breath.

12 Blessed is the man whom thou dost
   chasten, O LORD,
   and whom thou dost teach out of
   thy law
13 to give him respite from days of
   trouble,
   until a pit is dug for the wicked.
14 For the LORD will not forsake his
   people;
   he will not abandon his heritage;

15for justice will return to the righteous,
   and all the upright in heart will
   follow it.

16Who rises up for me against the
wicked?
   Who stands up for me against
   evildoers?
17If the LORD had not been my help,
   my soul would soon have dwelt in
   the land of silence.
18When I thought, "My foot slips,"
   thy steadfast love, O LORD, held
   me up.
19When the cares of my heart are
many,
   thy consolations cheer my soul.
20Can wicked rulers be allied with
thee,
   who frame mischief by statute?
21They band together against the life
   of the righteous,
   and condemn the innocent to
   death.
22But the LORD has become my
   stronghold,
   and my God the rock of my refuge.
23He will bring back on them their
   iniquity
   and wipe them out for their wickedness;
   the LORD our God will wipe them
   out.

95 O come, let us sing to the
LORD;
   let us make a joyful noise to the rock
   of our salvation!
2Let us come into his presence with
thanksgiving;
   let us make a joyful noise to him
   with songs of praise!
3For the LORD is a great God,
   and a great King above all gods.
4In his hand are the depths of the
earth;
   the heights of the mountains are
   his also.
5The sea is his, for he made it;
   for his hands formed the dry land.

6O come, let us worship and bow
down,

let us kneel before the LORD, our
Maker!
7For he is our God,
   and we are the people of his
   pasture,
   and the sheep of his hand.

O that today you would hearken to
   his voice!
8   Harden not your hearts, as at
   Mer'ibah,
   as on the day at Massah in the
   wilderness,
9when your fathers tested me,
   and put me to the proof, though
   they had seen my work.
10For forty years I loathed that generation
   and said, "They are a people who
   err in heart,
   and they do not regard my ways."
11Therefore I swore in my anger
   that they should not enter my rest.

96 O sing to the LORD a new song;
   sing to the LORD, all the earth!
2Sing to the LORD, bless his name;
   tell of his salvation from day to
   day.
3Declare his glory among the nations,
   his marvelous works among all
   the peoples!
4For great is the LORD, and greatly to
   be praised;
   he is to be feared above all gods.
5For all the gods of the peoples are
   idols;
   but the LORD made the heavens.
6Honor and majesty are before him;
   strength and beauty are in his
   sanctuary.

7Ascribe to the LORD, O families of
   the peoples,
   ascribe to the LORD glory and
   strength!
8Ascribe to the LORD the glory due
   his name;
   bring an offering, and come into
   his courts!
9Worship the LORD in holy array;
   tremble before him, all the earth!

10Say among the nations, "The LORD
   reigns!

Yea, the world is established, it
shall never be moved;
he will judge the peoples with
equity."
11 Let the heavens be glad, and let the
earth rejoice;
let the sea roar, and all that fills it;
12   let the field exult, and everything
in it!
Then shall all the trees of the wood
sing for joy
13   before the LORD, for he comes,
for he comes to judge the earth.
He will judge the world with righteousness,
and the peoples with his truth.

97 The LORD reigns; let the earth
rejoice;
let the many coastlands be glad!
2 Clouds and thick darkness are round
about him;
righteousness and justice are the
foundation of his throne.
3 Fire goes before him,
and burns up his adversaries
round about.
4 His lightnings lighten the world;
the earth sees and trembles.
5 The mountains melt like wax before
the LORD,
before the Lord of all the earth.

6 The heavens proclaim his righteousness;
and all the peoples behold his
glory.
7 All worshipers of images are put to
shame,
who make their boast in worthless
idols;
all gods bow down before him.
8 Zion hears and is glad,
and the daughters of Judah rejoice,
because of thy judgments, O God.
9 For thou, O LORD, art most high
over all the earth;
thou art exalted far above all gods.

10 The LORD loves those who hate evil;
he preserves the lives of his
saints;
he delivers them from the hand of
the wicked.

11 Light dawns for the righteous,
and joy for the upright in heart.

12 Rejoice in the LORD, O you righteous,
and give thanks to his holy name!

A Psalm.

98 O sing to the LORD a new song,
for he has done marvelous
things!
His right hand and his holy arm
have gotten him victory.
2 The LORD has made known his
victory,
he has revealed his vindication in
the sight of the nations.
3 He has remembered his steadfast
love and faithfulness
to the house of Israel.
All the ends of the earth have seen
the victory of our God.

4 Make a joyful noise to the LORD, all
the earth;
break forth into joyous song and
sing praises!
5 Sing praises to the LORD with the
lyre,
with the lyre and the sound of
melody!
6 With trumpets and the sound of the
horn
make a joyful noise before the
King, the LORD!

7 Let the sea roar, and all that fills it;
the world and those who dwell in
it!
8 Let the floods clap their hands;
let the hills sing for joy together
9 before the LORD, for he comes to
judge the earth.
He will judge the world with righteousness,
and the peoples with equity.

99 The LORD reigns; let the
peoples tremble!
He sits enthroned upon the
cherubim; let the earth quake!
2 The LORD is great in Zion;
he is exalted over all the peoples.

³ Let them praise thy great and terrible name!
Holy is he!
⁴ Mighty King, lover of justice,
thou hast established equity;
thou hast executed justice
and righteousness in Jacob.
⁵ Extol the LORD our God;
worship at his footstool!
Holy is he!

⁶ Moses and Aaron were among his priests,
Samuel also was among those who called on his name.
They cried to the LORD, and he answered them.
⁷ He spoke to them in the pillar of cloud;
they kept his testimonies,
and the statutes that he gave them.

⁸ O LORD our God, thou didst answer them;
thou wast a forgiving God to them,
but an avenger of their wrongdoings.
⁹ Extol the LORD our God,
and worship at his holy mountain;
for the LORD our God is holy!

A Psalm for the thank offering.

100 Make a joyful noise to the LORD, all the lands!
2 Serve the LORD with gladness!
Come into his presence with singing!

³ Know that the LORD is God!
It is he that made us, and we are his;
we are his people, and the sheep of his pasture.
⁴ Enter his gates with thanksgiving,
and his courts with praise!
Give thanks to him, bless his name!

⁵ For the LORD is good;
his steadfast love endures for ever,
and his faithfulness to all generations.

A Psalm of David.

101 I will sing of loyalty and of justice;
to thee, O LORD, I will sing.
² I will give heed to the way that is blameless.
Oh when wilt thou come to me?

I will walk with integrity of heart within my house;
³ I will not set before my eyes anything that is base.
I hate the work of those who fall away;
it shall not cleave to me.
⁴ Perverseness of heart shall be far from me;
I will know nothing of evil.

⁵ Him who slanders his neighbor secretly
I will destroy.
The man of haughty looks and arrogant heart
I will not endure.

⁶ I will look with favor on the faithful in the land,
that they may dwell with me;
he who walks in the way that is blameless
shall minister to me.
⁷ No man who practices deceit shall dwell in my house;
no man who utters lies shall continue in my presence.

⁸ Morning by morning I will destroy all the wicked in the land,
cutting off all the evildoers from the city of the LORD.

A prayer of one afflicted, when he is faint and pours out his complaint before the LORD.

102 Hear my prayer, O LORD; let my cry come to thee!
² Do not hide thy face from me in the day of my distress!
Incline thy ear to me;
answer me speedily in the day when I call!
³ For my days pass away like smoke,
and my bones burn like a furnace.

⁴My heart is smitten like grass, and
    withered;
  I forget to eat my bread.
⁵Because of my loud groaning
  my bones cleave to my flesh.
⁶I am like a vulture of the wilderness,
  like an owl of the waste places;
⁷I lie awake,
  I am like a lonely bird on the
    housetop.

⁸All the day my enemies taunt me,
  those who deride me use my
    name for a curse.
⁹For I eat ashes like bread,
  and mingle tears with my drink,
¹⁰because of thy indignation and
    anger;
  for thou hast taken me up and
    thrown me away.
¹¹My days are like an evening
    shadow;
  I wither away like grass.

¹²But thou, O LORD, art enthroned for
    ever;
  thy name endures to all genera-
    tions.
¹³Thou wilt arise and have pity on
    Zion;
  it is the time to favor her;
  the appointed time has come.
¹⁴For thy servants hold her stones
    dear;
  and have pity on her dust.
¹⁵The nations will fear the name of the
    LORD,
  and all the kings of the earth thy
    glory.
¹⁶For the LORD will build up Zion,
  he will appear in his glory;
¹⁷he will regard the prayer of the des-
    titute,
  and will not despise their suppli-
    cation.

¹⁸Let this be recorded for a generation
    to come,
  so that a people yet unborn may
    praise the LORD:
¹⁹that he looked down from his holy
    height,
  from heaven the LORD looked at
    the earth,
²⁰to hear the groans of the prisoners,
  to set free those who were
    doomed to die;

²¹that men may declare in Zion the
    name of the LORD,
  and in Jerusalem his praise,
²²when peoples gather together,
  and kingdoms, to worship the
    LORD.

²³He has broken my strength in mid-
    course;
  he has shortened my days.
²⁴"O my God," I say, "take me not
    hence
  in the midst of my days,
  thou whose years endure
    throughout all generations!"

²⁵Of old thou didst lay the foundation
    of the earth,
  and the heavens are the work of
    thy hands.
²⁶They will perish, but thou dost en-
    dure;
  they will all wear out like a gar-
    ment.
  Thou changest them like raiment,
    and they pass away;
²⁷ but thou art the same, and thy
    years have no end.

²⁸The children of thy servants shall
    dwell secure;
  their posterity shall be established
    before thee.

A Psalm of David.

103 Bless the LORD, O my soul;
  and all that is within me,
  bless his holy name!
²Bless the LORD, O my soul,
  and forget not all his benefits,
³who forgives all your iniquity,
  who heals all your diseases,
⁴who redeems your life from the Pit,
  who crowns you with steadfast
    love and mercy,
⁵who satisfies you with good as long
    as you live
  so that your youth is renewed like
    the eagle's.

⁶The LORD works vindication
  and justice for all who are op-
    pressed.
⁷He made known his ways to Moses,
  his acts to the people of Israel.

⁸ The LORD is merciful and gracious,
    slow to anger and abounding in
    steadfast love.
⁹ He will not always chide,
    nor will he keep his anger for ever.
¹⁰ He does not deal with us according
    to our sins,
    nor requite us according to our in-
    iquities.
¹¹ For as the heavens are high above
    the earth,
    so great is his steadfast love
    toward those who fear him;
¹² as far as the east is from the west,
    so far does he remove our
    transgressions from us.
¹³ As a father pities his children,
    so the LORD pities those who fear
    him.
¹⁴ For he knows our frame;
    he remembers that we are dust.

¹⁵ As for man, his days are like grass;
    he flourishes like a flower of the
    field;
¹⁶ for the wind passes over it, and it is
    gone,
    and its place knows it no more.
¹⁷ But the steadfast love of the LORD is
    from everlasting to everlasting
    upon those who fear him,
    and his righteousness to chil-
    dren's children,
¹⁸ to those who keep his covenant
    and remember to do his com-
    mandments.

¹⁹ The LORD has established his throne
    in the heavens,
    and his kingdom rules over all.
²⁰ Bless the LORD, O you his angels,
    you mighty ones who do his
    word,
    hearkening to the voice of his
    word!
²¹ Bless the LORD, all his hosts,
    his ministers that do his will!
²² Bless the LORD, all his works,
    in all places of his dominion.
    Bless the LORD, O my soul!

104 Bless the LORD, O my soul!
    O LORD my God, thou art
    very great!
Thou art clothed with honor and
    majesty,

² who coverest thyself with light as
    with a garment,
who hast stretched out the heavens
    like a tent,
³ who hast laid the beams of thy
    chambers on the waters,
who makest the clouds thy chariot,
    who ridest on the wings of the
    wind,
⁴ who makest the winds thy messen-
    gers,
    fire and flame thy ministers.

⁵ Thou didst set the earth on its foun-
    dations,
    so that it should never be shaken.
⁶ Thou didst cover it with the deep as
    with a garment;
    the waters stood above the
    mountains.
⁷ At thy rebuke they fled;
    at the sound of thy thunder they
    took to flight.
⁸ The mountains rose, the valleys
    sank down
    to the place which thou didst ap-
    point for them.
⁹ Thou didst set a bound which they
    should not pass,
    so that they might not again cover
    the earth.

¹⁰ Thou makest springs gush forth in
    the valleys;
    they flow between the hills,
¹¹ they give drink to every beast of the
    field;
    the wild asses quench their thirst.
¹² By them the birds of the air have
    their habitation;
    they sing among the branches.
¹³ From thy lofty abode thou waterest
    the mountains;
    the earth is satisifed with the fruit
    of thy work.
¹⁴ Thou dost cause the grass to grow
    for the cattle,
    and plants for man to cultivate,
    that he may bring forth food from
    the earth,
¹⁵ and wine to gladden the heart of
    man,
    oil to make his face shine,
    and bread to strengthen man's
    heart.
¹⁶ The trees of the LORD are watered
    abundantly,

the cedars of Lebanon which he
planted.
[17]In them the birds build their nests;
the stork has her home in the fir
trees.
[18]The high mountains are for the wild
goats;
the rocks are a refuge for the bad-
gers.

[19]Thou hast made the moon to mark
the seasons;
the sun knows its time for setting.
[20]Thou makest darkness, and it is
night,
when all the beasts of the forest
creep forth.
[21]The young lions roar for their prey,
seeking their food from God.
[22]When the sun rises, they get them
away
and lie down in their dens.
[23]Man goes forth to his work
and to his labor until the evening.

[24]O LORD, how manifold are thy
works!
In wisdom hast thou made them
all;
the earth is full of thy creatures.
[25]Yonder is the sea, great and wide,
which teems with things innum-
erable,
living things both small and great.
[26]There go the ships,
and Leviathan which thou didst
form to sport in it.

[27]These all look to thee,
to give them their food in due season.
[28]When thou givest to them, they
gather it up;
when thou openest thy hand,
they are filled with good things.
[29]When thou hidest thy face, they are
dismayed;
when thou takest away their
breath, they die
and return to their dust.
[30]When thou sendest forth thy Spirit,
they are created;
and thou renewest the face of the
ground.

[31]May the glory of the LORD endure
for ever,
may the LORD rejoice in his
works,
[32]who looks on the earth and it trembles,
who touches the mountains and
they smoke!
[33]I will sing to the LORD as long as I
live;
I will sing praise to my God while
I have being.
[34]May my meditation be pleasing to
him,
for I rejoice in the LORD.
[35]Let sinners be consumed from the
earth,
and let the wicked be no more!
Bless the LORD, O my soul!
Praise the LORD!

105 O give thanks to the LORD,
call on his name,
make known his deeds among the
peoples!
[2]Sing to him, sing praises to him,
tell of all his wonderful works!
[3]Glory in his holy name;
let the hearts of those who seek
the LORD rejoice!
[4]Seek the LORD and his strength,
seek his presence continually!
[5]Remember the wonderful works
that he has done,
his miracles, and the judgments
he uttered,
[6]O offspring of Abraham his servant,
sons of Jacob, his chosen ones!

[7]He is the LORD our God;
his judgments are in all the earth.
[8]He is mindful of his covenant for
ever,
of the word that he commanded,
for a thousand generations,
[9]the covenant which he made with
Abraham,
his sworn promise to Isaac,
[10]which he confirmed to Jacob as a
statute,
to Israel as an everlasting covenant,
[11]saying, "To you I will give the land
of Canaan
as your portion for an inheritance."

12 When they were few in number,
    of little account, and sojourners in
        it,
13 wandering from nation to nation,
    from one kingdom to another
        people,
14 he allowed no one to oppress them;
    he rebuked kings on their ac-
        count,
15 saying, "Touch not my anointed
        ones,
    do my prophets no harm!"

16 When he summoned a famine on
        the land,
    and broke every staff of bread,
17 he had sent a man ahead of them,
    Joseph, who was sold as a slave.
18 His feet were hurt with fetters,
    his neck was put in a collar of
        iron;
19 until what he had said came to pass
    the word of the LORD tested him.
20 The king sent and released him,
    the ruler of the peoples set him
        free;
21 he made him lord of his house,
    and ruler of all his possessions,
22 to instruct his princes at his plea-
        sure,
    and to teach his elders wisdom.

23 Then Israel came to Egypt;
    Jacob sojourned in the land of
        Ham.
24 And the LORD made his people very
        fruitful,
    and made them stronger than
        their foes.
25 He turned their hearts to hate his
        people,
    to deal craftily with his servants.

26 He sent Moses his servant,
    and Aaron whom he had chosen.
27 They wrought his signs among
        them,
    and miracles in the land of Ham.

28 He sent darkness, and made the
        land dark;
    they rebelled against his words.
29 He turned their waters into blood,
    and caused their fish to die.
30 Their land swarmed with frogs,
    even in the chambers of their
        kings.

31 He spoke, and there came swarms of
        flies,
    and gnats throughout their coun-
        try.
32 He gave them hail for rain,
    and lightning that flashed
        through their land.
33 He smote their vines and fig trees,
    and shattered the trees of their
        country.
34 He spoke, and the locusts came,
    and young locusts without
        number;
35 which devoured all the vegetation in
        their land,
    and ate up the fruit of their
        ground.
36 He smote all the first-born in their
        land,
    the first issue of all their strength.

37 Then he led forth Israel with silver
        and gold,
    and there was none among his
        tribes who stumbled.
38 Egypt was glad when they departed,
    for dread of them had fallen upon
        it.
39 He spread a cloud for a covering,
    and fire to give light by night.
40 They asked, and he brought quails,
    and gave them bread from heaven
        in abundance.
41 He opened the rock, and water
        gushed forth;
    it flowed through the desert like a
        river.
42 For he remembered his holy prom-
        ise,
    and Abraham his servant.

43 So he led forth his people with joy,
    his chosen ones with singing.
44 And he gave them the lands of the
        nations;
    and they took possession of the
        fruit of the peoples' toil,
45 to the end that they should keep his
        statutes,
    and observe his laws.
Praise the LORD!

106 Praise the LORD!
    O give thanks to the LORD,
        for he is good;

for his steadfast love endures for
ever!
² Who can utter the mighty doings of
the LORD,
or show forth all his praise!
³ Blessed are they who observe justice,
who do righteousness at all times!

⁴ Remember me, O LORD, when thou
showest favor to thy people;
help me when thou deliverest
them;
⁵ that I may see the prosperity of thy
chosen ones,
that I may rejoice in the gladness
of thy nation,
that I may glory with thy heritage.
⁶ Both we and our fathers have
sinned;
we have committed iniquity, we
have done wickedly.
⁷ Our fathers, when they were in
Egypt,
did not consider thy wonderful
works;
they did not remember the abundance of thy steadfast love,
but rebelled against the Most
High at the Red Sea.
⁸ Yet he saved them for his name's
sake,
that he might make known his
mighty power.
⁹ He rebuked the Red Sea, and it became dry;
and he led them through the deep
as through a desert.
¹⁰ So he saved them from the hand of
the foe,
and delivered them from the
power of the enemy.
¹¹ And the waters covered their adversaries;
not one of them was left.
¹² Then they believed his words;
they sang his praise.

¹³ But they soon forgot his works;
they did not wait for his counsel.
¹⁴ But they had a wanton craving in
the wilderness,
and put God to the test in the desert;
¹⁵ he gave them what they asked,
but sent a wasting disease among
them.

¹⁶ When men in the camp were jealous
of Moses
and Aaron, the holy one of the
LORD,
¹⁷ the earth opened and swallowed up
Dathan,
and covered the company of
Abi'ram.
¹⁸ Fire also broke out in their company;
the flame burned up the wicked.

¹⁹ They made a calf in Horeb
and worshiped a molten image.
²⁰ They exchanged the glory of God
for the image of an ox that eats
grass.
²¹ They forgot God, their Savior,
who had done great things in
Egypt,
²² wondrous works in the land of
Ham,
and terrible things by the Red
Sea.

²³ Therefore he said he would destroy
them—
had not Moses, his chosen one,
stood in the breach before him,
to turn away his wrath from destroying them.

²⁴ Then they despised the pleasant
land,
having no faith in his promise.
²⁵ They murmured in their tents,
and did not obey the voice of the
LORD.
²⁶ Therefore he raised his hand and
swore to them
that he would make them fall in
the wilderness,
²⁷ and would disperse their descendants among the nations,
scattering them over the lands.

²⁸ Then they attached themselves to
the Ba'al of Pe'or,
and ate sacrifices offered to the
dead;
²⁹ they provoked the LORD to anger
with their doings,
and a plague broke out among
them.
³⁰ Then Phin'ehas stood up and inter-
posed,
and the plague was stayed.

31 And that has been reckoned to him
   as righteousness
   from generation to generation for
   ever.

32 They angered him at the waters of
   Mer'ibah,
   and it went ill with Moses on their
   account;
33 for they made his spirit bitter,
   and he spoke words that were
   rash.

34 They did not destroy the peoples,
   as the LORD commanded them,
35 but they mingled with the nations
   and learned to do as they did.
36 They served their idols,
   which became a snare to them.
37 They sacrificed their sons
   and their daughters to the de-
   mons;
38 they poured out innocent blood,
   the blood of their sons and
   daughters,
   whom they sacrificed to the idols of
   Canaan;
   and the land was polluted with
   blood.
39 Thus they became unclean by their
   acts,
   and played the harlot in their doings.

40 Then the anger of the LORD was
   kindled against his people,
   and he abhorred his heritage;
41 he gave them into the hand of the
   nations,
   so that those who hated them
   ruled over them.
42 Their enemies oppressed them,
   and they were brought into sub-
   jection under their power.

43 Many times he delivered them,
   but they were rebellious in their
   purposes,
   and were brought low through
   their iniquity.
44 Nevertheless he regarded their distress,
   when he heard their cry.
45 He remembered for their sake his
   covenant,
   and relented according to the
   abundance of his steadfast love.

46 He caused them to be pitied
   by all those who held them cap-
   tive.

47 Save us, O LORD our God,
   and gather us from among the nations,
   that we may give thanks to thy holy
   name
   and glory in thy praise.

48 Blessed be the LORD, the God of Israel,
   from everlasting to everlasting!
   And let all the people say, "Amen!"
   Praise the LORD!

BOOK V

107 O give thanks to the LORD,
   for he is good;
   for his steadfast love endures for
   ever!
2 Let the redeemed of the LORD say
   so,
   whom he has redeemed from
   trouble
3 and gathered in from the lands,
   from the east and from the west,
   from the north and from the
   south.

4 Some wandered in desert wastes,
   finding no way to a city to dwell
   in;
5 hungry and thirsty,
   their soul fainted within them.
6 Then they cried to the LORD in their
   trouble,
   and he delivered them from their
   distress;
7 he led them by a straight way,
   till they reached a city to dwell in.
8 Let them thank the LORD for his
   steadfast love,
   for his wonderful works to the
   sons of men!
9 For he satisfies him who is thirsty,
   and the hungry he fills with good
   things.

10 Some sat in darkness and in gloom,
   prisoners in affliction and in
   irons,

11 for they had rebelled against the words of God,
and spurned the counsel of the Most High.
12 Their hearts were bowed down with hard labor;
they fell down, with none to help.
13 Then they cried to the LORD in their trouble,
and he delivered them from their distress;
14 he brought them out of darkness and gloom,
and broke their bonds asunder.

15 Let them thank the LORD for his steadfast love,
for his wonderful works to the sons of men!
16 For he shatters the doors of bronze,
and cuts in two the bars of iron.

17 Some were sick through their sinful ways,
and because of their iniquities suffered affliction;
18 they loathed any kind of food,
and they drew near to the gates of death.
19 Then they cried to the LORD in their trouble,
and he delivered them from their distress;
20 he sent forth his word, and healed them,
and delivered them from destruction.
21 Let them thank the LORD for his steadfast love,
for his wonderful works to the sons of men!
22 And let them offer sacrifices of thanksgiving,
and tell of his deeds in songs of joy!

23 Some went down to the sea in ships,
doing business on the great waters;
24 they saw the deeds of the LORD,
his wondrous works in the deep.
25 For he commanded, and raised the stormy wind,
which lifted up the waves of the sea.
26 They mounted up to heaven, they went down to the depths;

their courage melted away in their evil plight;
27 they reeled and staggered like drunken men,
and were at their wits' end.
28 Then they cried to the LORD in their trouble
and he delivered them from their distress;
29 he made the storm be still,
and the waves of the sea were hushed.
30 Then they were glad because they had quiet,
and he brought them to their desired haven.
31 Let them thank the LORD for his steadfast love,
for his wonderful works to the sons of men!
32 Let them extol him in the congregation of the people,
and praise him in the assembly of the elders.

33 He turns rivers into a desert,
springs of water into thirsty ground,
34 a fruitful land into a salty waste,
because of the wickedness of its inhabitants.
35 He turns a desert into pools of water,
a parched land into springs of water.
36 And there he lets the hungry dwell,
and they establish a city to live in;
37 they sow fields, and plant vineyards,
and get a fruitful yield.
38 By his blessing they multiply greatly;
and he does not let their cattle decrease.
39 When they are diminished and brought low
through oppression, trouble, and sorrow,
40 he pours contempt upon princes
and makes them wander in trackless wastes;
41 but he raises up the needy out of affliction,
and makes their families like flocks.
42 The upright see it and are glad;
and all wickedness stops its mouth.

43 Whoever is wise, let him give heed
to these things;
let men consider the steadfast love
of the LORD.

A Song. A Psalm of David.

108

My heart is steadfast, O God,
my heart is steadfast!
I will sing and make melody!
Awake, my soul!
2 Awake, O harp and lyre!
I will awake the dawn!
3 I will give thanks to thee, O LORD,
among the peoples,
I will sing praises to thee among
the nations.
4 For thy steadfast love is great above
the heavens,
thy faithfulness reaches to the
clouds.
5 Be exalted, O God, above the heavens!
Let thy glory be over all the earth!
6 That thy beloved may be delivered,
give help by thy right hand, and
answer me!

7 God has promised in his sanctuary:
"With exultation I will divide up
Shechem,
and portion out the Vale of Suc-
coth.
8 Gilead is mine; Manas'seh is mine;
E'phraim is my helmet;
Judah my scepter.
9 Moab is my washbasin;
upon Edom I cast my shoe;
over Philistia I shout in triumph."
10 Who will bring me to the fortified
city?
Who will lead me to Edom?
11 Hast thou not rejected us, O God?
Thou dost not go forth, O God,
with our armies.
12 O grant us help against the foe,
for vain is the help of man!
13 With God we shall do valiantly;
it is he who will tread down our
foes.

To the choirmaster. A Psalm of David.

109

Be not silent, O God of my
praise!

2 For wicked and deceitful mouths are
opened against me,
speaking against me with lying
tongues.
3 They beset me with words of hate,
and attack me without cause.
4 In return for my love they accuse
me,
even as I make prayer for them.
5 So they reward me evil for good,
and hatred for my love.

6 Appoint a wicked man against him;
let an accuser bring him to trial.
7 When he is tried, let him come forth
guilty;
let his prayer be counted as sin!
8 May his days be few;
may another seize his goods!
9 May his children be fatherless,
and his wife a widow!
10 May his children wander about and
beg;
may they be driven out of the
ruins they inhabit!
11 May the creditor seize all that he
has;
may strangers plunder the fruits
of his toil!

12 Let there be none to extend kindness to him,
nor any to pity his fatherless children!
13 May his posterity be cut off;
may his name be blotted out in
the second generation!
14 May the iniquity of his fathers be
remembered before the LORD,
and let not the sin of his mother
be blotted out!
15 Let them be before the LORD continually;
and may his memory be cut off
from the earth!

16 For he did not remember to show
kindness,
but pursued the poor and needy
and the brokenhearted to their
death.
17 He loved to curse; let curses come on
him!
He did not like blessing; may it be
far from him!
18 He clothed himself with cursing as
his coat,

may it soak into his body like water,
like oil into his bones!
[19] May it be like a garment which he
wraps round him,
like a belt with which he daily
girds himself!

[20] May this be the reward of my accusers from the LORD,
of those who speak evil against
my life!
[21] But thou, O GOD my Lord,
deal on my behalf for thy name's
sake;
because thy steadfast love is good,
deliver me!
[22] For I am poor and needy,
and my heart is stricken within
me.
[23] I am gone, like a shadow at evening;
I am shaken off like a locust.
[24] My knees are weak through fasting;
my body has become gaunt.
[25] I am an object of scorn to my accusers;
when they see me, they wag their
heads.
[26] Help me, O LORD my God!
Save me according to thy steadfast
love!
[27] Let them know that this is thy hand;
thou, O LORD, hast done it!
[28] Let them curse, but do thou bless!
Let my assailants be put to shame;
may thy servant be glad!
[29] May my accusers be clothed with
dishonor;
may they be wrapped in their
own shame as in a mantle!

[30] With my mouth I will give great
thanks to the LORD;
I will praise him in the midst of
the throng.
[31] For he stands at the right hand of the
needy,
to save him from those who condemn him to death.

A Psalm of David.

110 The LORD says to my lord:
"Sit at my right hand,
till I make your enemies
your footstool."

[2] The LORD sends forth from Zion
your mighty scepter.
Rule in the midst of your foes!
[3] Your people will offer themselves
freely
on the day you lead your host
upon the holy mountains.
From the womb of the morning
like dew your youth will come to
you.

[4] The LORD has sworn
and will not change his mind,
"You are a priest for ever
after the order of Melchiz'edek."

[5] The Lord is at your right hand;
he will shatter kings on the day of
his wrath.
[6] He will execute judgment among the
nations,
filling them with corpses;
he will shatter chiefs
over the wide earth.
[7] He will drink from the brook by the
way;
therefore he will lift up his head.

111 Praise the LORD.
I will give thanks to the LORD
with my whole heart,
in the company of the upright,
in the congregation.
[2] Great are the works of the LORD,
studied by all who have pleasure
in them.
[3] Full of honor and majesty is his
work,
and his righteousness endures for
ever.
[4] He has caused his wonderful works
to be remembered;
the LORD is gracious and merciful.
[5] He provides food for those who fear
him;
he is ever mindful of his covenant.
[6] He has shown his people the power
of his works,
in giving them the heritage of the
nations.
[7] The works of his hands are faithful
and just;
all his precepts are trustworthy,

8 they are established for ever and
ever,
to be performed with faithfulness
and uprightness.
9 He sent redemption to his people;
he has commanded his covenant
for ever.
Holy and terrible is his name!
10 The fear of the LORD is the beginning of wisdom;
a good understanding have all
those who practice it.
His praise endures for ever!

112 Praise the LORD.
Blessed is the man who fears
the LORD,
who greatly delights in his commandments!
2 His descendants will be mighty in
the land;
the generation of the upright will
be blessed.
3 Wealth and riches are in his house;
and his righteousness endures for
ever.
4 Light rises in the darkness for the
upright;
the LORD is gracious, merciful,
and righteous.
5 It is well with the man who deals
generously and lends,
who conducts his affairs with justice.
6 For the righteous will never be
moved;
he will be remembered for ever.
7 He is not afraid of evil tidings;
his heart is firm, trusting in the
LORD.
8 His heart is steady, he will not be
afraid,
until he sees his desire on his adversaries.
9 He has distributed freely, he has
given to the poor;
his righteousness endures for
ever;
his horn is exalted in honor.
10 The wicked man sees it and is angry;
he gnashes his teeth and melts
away;
the desire of the wicked man
comes to nought.

113 Praise the LORD!
Praise, O servants of the
LORD,
praise the name of the LORD!

2 Blessed be the name of the LORD
from his time forth and for evermore!
3 From the rising of the sun to its setting
the name of the LORD is to be
praised!
4 The LORD is high above all nations,
and his glory above the heavens!

5 Who is like the LORD our God,
who is seated on high,
6 who looks far down
upon the heavens and the earth?

7 He raises the poor from the dust,
and lifts the needy from the ash
heap,
8 to make them sit with princes,
with the princes of his people.
9 He gives the barren woman a home,
making her the joyous mother of
children.
Praise the LORD!

114 When Israel went forth from
Egypt,
the house of Jacob from a people
of strange language,
2 Judah became his sanctuary,
Israel his dominion.

3 The sea looked and fled,
Jordan turned back.
4 The mountains skipped like rams,
the hills like lambs.

5 What ails you, O sea, that you flee?
O Jordan, that you turn back?
6 O mountains, that you skip like
rams?
O hills, like lambs?

7 Tremble, O earth, at the presence of
the LORD,
at the presence of the God of
Jacob,
8 who turns the rock into a pool of
water,
the flint into a spring of water.

115

Not to us, O LORD, not to us,
but to thy name give glory,
for the sake of thy steadfast love
and thy faithfulness!
2 Why should the nations say,
"Where is their God?"

3 Our God is in the heavens;
he does whatever he pleases.
4 Their idols are silver and gold,
the work of men's hands.
5 They have mouths, but do not
speak;
eyes, but do not see.
6 They have ears, but do not hear;
noses, but do not smell.
7 They have hands, but do not feel;
feet, but do not walk;
and they do not make a sound in
their throat.
8 Those who make them are like
them;
so are all who trust in them.

9 O Israel, trust in the LORD!
He is their help and their shield.
10 O house of Aaron, put your trust in
the LORD!
He is their help and their shield.
11 You who fear the LORD, trust in the
LORD!
He is their help and their shield.

12 The LORD has been mindful of us;
he will bless us;
he will bless the house of Israel;
he will bless the house of Aaron;
13 he will bless those who fear the
LORD,
both small and great.

14 May the LORD give you increase,
you and your children!
15 May you be blessed by the LORD,
who made heaven and earth!

16 The heavens are the LORD's heavens,
but the earth he has given to the
sons of men.
17 The dead do not praise the LORD,
nor do any that go down into silence.
18 But we will bless the LORD from
this time forth and for evermore.
Praise the LORD!

116

I love the LORD, because he
has heard
my voice and my supplications.
2 Because he inclined his ear to me,
therefore I will call on him as long
as I live.
3 The snares of death encompassed
me;
the pangs of Sheol laid hold on
me;
I suffered distress and anguish.
4 Then I called on the name of the
LORD:
"O LORD, I beseech thee, save my
life!"

5 Gracious is the LORD, and righteous;
our God is merciful.
6 The LORD preserves the simple;
when I was brought low, he saved
me.
7 Return, O my soul, to your rest;
for the LORD has dealt bountifully
with you.
8 For thou hast delivered my soul
from death,
my eyes from tears,
my feet from stumbling;
9 I walk before the LORD
in the land of the living.
10 I kept my faith, even when I said,
"I am greatly afflicted";
11 I said in my consternation,
"Men are all a vain hope."

12 What shall I render to the LORD
for all his bounty to me?
13 I will lift up the cup of salvation
and call on the name of the LORD,
14 I will pay my vows to the LORD
in the presence of all his people.
15 Precious in the sight of the LORD
is the death of his saints.
16 O LORD, I am thy servant;
I am thy servant, the son of thy
handmaid.
Thou hast loosed my bonds.
17 I will offer to thee the sacrifice of
thanksgiving
and call on the name of the LORD.
18 I will pay my vows to the LORD
in the presence of all his people,
19 in the courts of the house of the
LORD,
in your midst, O Jerusalem.
Praise the LORD!

117 Praise the LORD all nations!
Extol him, all peoples!
2 For great is his steadfast love toward
us;
and the faithfulness of the LORD
endures for ever.
Praise the LORD!

118 O give thanks to the LORD,
for he is good;
his steadfast love endures for
ever!
2 Let Israel say,
"His steadfast love endures for
ever."
3 Let the house of Aaron say,
"His steadfast love endures for
ever."
4 Let those who fear the LORD say,
"His steadfast love endures for
ever."

5 Out of my distress I called on the
LORD;
the LORD answered me and set me
free.
6 With the LORD on my side I do not
fear.
What can man do to me?
7 The LORD is on my side to help me;
I shall look in triumph on those
who hate me.
8 It is better to take refuge in the LORD
than to put confidence in man.
9 It is better to take refuge in the LORD
than to put confidence in
princes.

10 All nations surrounded me;
in the name of the LORD I cut
them off!
11 They surrounded me, surrounded
me on every side;
in the name of the LORD I cut
them off!
12 They surrounded me like bees,
they blazed like a fire of thorns;
in the name of the LORD I cut
them off!
13 I was pushed hard, so that I was
falling,
but the LORD helped me.
14 The LORD is my strength and my
song;
he has become my salvation.

15 Hark, glad songs of victory
in the tents of the righteous:
"The right hand of the LORD does
valiantly,
16 the right hand of the LORD is
exalted,
the right hand of the LORD does
valiantly!"
17 I shall not die, but I shall live,
and recount the deeds of the
LORD.
18 The LORD has chastened me sorely,
but he has not given me over to
death.

19 Open to me the gates of righteousness,
that I may enter through them
and give thanks to the LORD.
20 This is the gate of the LORD;
the righteous shall enter through
it.

21 I thank thee that thou hast answered
me
and hast become my salvation.
22 The stone which the builders rejected
has become the head of the corner.
23 This is the LORD's doing;
it is marvelous in our eyes.
24 This is the day which the LORD has
made;
let us rejoice and be glad in it.
25 Save us, we beseech thee, O LORD!
O LORD, we beseech thee, give us
success!

26 Blessed be he who enters in the
name of the LORD!
We bless you from the house of
the LORD.
27 The LORD is God,
and he has given us light.
Bind the festal procession with
branches,
up to the horns of the altar!

28 Thou art my God, and I will give
thanks to thee;
thou art my God, I will extol thee.

29 O give thanks to the LORD, for he is
good;
for his steadfast love endures for
ever!

119

Blessed are those whose way is blameless,
who walk in the law of the LORD!
2 Blessed are those who keep his testimonies,
who seek him with their whole heart,
3 who also do no wrong,
but walk in his ways!
4 Thou hast commanded thy precepts
to be kept diligently.
5 O that my ways may be steadfast
in keeping thy statutes!
6 Then I shall not be put to shame,
having my eyes fixed on all thy commandments.
7 I will praise thee with an upright heart,
when I learn thy righteous ordinances.
8 I will observe thy statutes;
O forsake me not utterly!

9 How can a young man keep his way pure?
By guarding it according to thy word.
10 With my whole heart I seek thee;
let me not wander from thy commandments!
11 I have laid up thy word in my heart,
that I might not sin against thee.
12 Blessed be thou, O LORD;
teach me thy statutes!
13 With my lips I declare
all the ordinances of thy mouth.
14 In the way of thy testimonies I delight
as much as in all riches.
15 I will meditate on thy precepts,
and fix my eyes on thy ways.
16 I will delight in thy statutes;
I will not forget thy word.

17 Deal bountifully with thy servant,
that I may live and observe thy word.
18 Open my eyes, that I may behold
wondrous things out of thy law.
19 I am a sojourner on earth;
hide not thy commandments from me!
20 My soul is consumed with longing
for thy ordinances at all times.
21 Thou dost rebuke the insolent, accursed ones,
who wander from thy commandments;
22 take away from me their scorn and contempt,
for I have kept thy testimonies.
23 Even though princes sit plotting against me,
thy servant will meditate on thy statutes.
24 Thy testimonies are my delight,
they are my counselors.

25 My soul cleaves to the dust;
revive me according to thy word!
26 When I told of my ways, thou didst answer me;
teach me thy statutes!
27 Make me understand the way of thy precepts,
and I will meditate on thy wondrous works.
28 My soul melts away for sorrow;
strengthen me according to thy word!
29 Put false ways far from me;
and graciously teach me thy law!
30 I have chosen the way of faithfulness,
I set thy ordinances before me.
31 I cleave to thy testimonies, O LORD;
let me not be put to shame!
32 I will run in the way of thy commandments
when thou enlargest my understanding!

33 Teach me, O LORD, the way of thy statutes;
and I will keep it to the end.
34 Give me understanding, that I may keep thy law
and observe it with my whole heart.
35 Lead me in the path of thy commandments,
for I delight in it.
36 Incline my heart to thy testimonies,
and not to gain!
37 Turn my eyes from looking at vanities;
and give me life in thy ways.
38 Confirm to thy servant thy promise,
which is for those who fear thee.
39 Turn away the reproach which I dread;
for thy ordinances are good.

40 Behold, I long for thy precepts;
in thy righteousness give me life!
41 Let thy steadfast love come to me, O
LORD,
thy salvation according to thy
promise;
42 then shall I have an answer for those
who taunt me,
for I trust in thy word.
43 And take not the word of truth utterly out of my mouth,
for my hope is in thy ordinances.
44 I will keep thy law continually,
for ever and ever;
45 and I shall walk at liberty,
for I have sought thy precepts.
46 I will also speak of thy testimonies
before kings,
and shall not be put to shame;
47 for I find my delight in thy commandments,
which I love.
48 I revere thy commandments, which I
love,
and I will meditate on thy statutes.

49 Remember thy word to thy servant,
in which thou hast made me
hope.
50 This is my comfort in my affliction
that thy promise gives me life.
51 Godless men utterly deride me,
but I do not turn away from thy
law.
52 When I think of thy ordinances from
of old,
I take comfort, O LORD.
53 Hot indignation seizes me because
of the wicked,
who forsake thy law.
54 Thy statutes have been my songs
in the house of my pilgrimage.
55 I remember thy name in the night,
O LORD,
and keep thy law.
56 This blessing has fallen to me,
that I have kept thy precepts.

57 The LORD is my portion;
I promise to keep thy words.
58 I entreat thy favor with all my heart;
be gracious to me according to thy
promise.
59 When I think of thy ways,
I turn my feet to thy testimonies;

60 I hasten and do not delay
to keep thy commandments.
61 Though the cords of the wicked en-
snare me,
I do not forget thy law.
62 At midnight I rise to praise thee,
because of thy righteous ordinances.
63 I am a companion of all who fear
thee,
of those who keep thy precepts.
64 The earth, O LORD, is full of thy
steadfast love;
teach me thy statutes!

65 Thou hast dealt well with thy servant,
O LORD, according to thy word.
66 Teach me good judgment and
knowledge,
for I believe in thy commandments.
67 Before I was afflicted I went astray;
but now I keep thy word.
68 Thou art good and doest good;
teach me thy statutes.
69 The godless besmear me with lies,
but with my whole heart I keep
thy precepts;
70 their heart is gross like fat,
but I delight in thy law.
71 It is good for me that I was afflicted,
that I might learn thy statutes.
72 The law of thy mouth is better to me
than thousands of gold and silver
pieces.

73 Thy hands have made and fash-
ioned me;
give me understanding that I may
learn thy commandments.
74 Those who fear thee shall see me
and rejoice,
because I have hoped in thy word.
75 I know, O LORD, that thy judgments
are right,
and that in faithfulness thou hast
afflicted me.
76 Let thy steadfast love be ready to
comfort me
according to thy promise to thy
servant.
77 Let thy mercy come to me, that I
may live;
for thy law is my delight.
78 Let the godless be put to shame,

because they have subverted me
   with guile;
   as for me, I will meditate on thy
   precepts.
79 Let those who fear thee turn to me,
   that they may know thy testimonies.
80 May my heart be blameless in thy
   statutes,
   that I may not be put to shame!

81 My soul languishes for thy salvation;
   I hope in thy word.
82 My eyes fail with watching for thy
   promise;
   I ask, "When wilt thou comfort
   me?"
83 For I have become like a wineskin in
   the smoke,
   yet I have not forgotten thy statutes.
84 How long must thy servant endure?
   When wilt thou judge those who
   persecute me?
85 Godless men have dug pitfalls for
   me,
   men who do not conform to thy
   law.
86 All thy commandments are sure;
   they persecute me with falsehood;
   help me!
87 They have almost made an end of
   me on earth;
   but I have not forsaken thy precepts.
88 In thy steadfast love spare my life,
   that I may keep the testimonies of
   thy mouth.

89 For ever, O LORD, thy word
   is firmly fixed in the heavens.
90 Thy faithfulness endures to all generations;
   thou hast established the earth,
   and it stands fast.
91 By thy appointment they stand this
   day;
   for all things are thy servants.
92 If thy law had not been my delight,
   I should have perished in my
   affliction.
93 I will never forget thy precepts;
   for by them thou hast given me
   life.
94 I am thine, save me;
   for I have sought thy precepts.

95 The wicked lie in wait to destroy
   me;
   but I consider thy testimonies.
96 I have seen a limit to all perfection,
   but thy commandment is exceedingly broad.

97 Oh, how I love thy law!
   It is my meditation all the day.
98 Thy commandment makes me wiser
   than my enemies,
   for it is ever with me.
99 I have more understanding than all
   my teachers,
   for thy testimonies are my meditation.
100 I understand more than the aged,
   for I keep thy precepts.
101 I hold back my feet from every evil
   way,
   in order to keep thy word.
102 I do not turn aside from thy ordinances,
   for thou hast taught me.
103 How sweet are thy words to my
   taste,
   sweeter than honey to my
   mouth!
104 Through thy precepts I get understanding;
   therefore I hate every false way.

105 Thy word is a lamp to my feet
   and a light to my path.
106 I have sworn an oath and confirmed it,
   to observe thy righteous ordinances.
107 I am sorely afflicted;
   give me life, O LORD, according
   to thy word!
108 Accept my offerings of praise, O
   LORD,
   and teach me thy ordinances.
109 I hold my life in my hand continually,
   but I do not forget thy law.
110 The wicked have laid a snare for
   me,
   but I do not stray from thy precepts.
111 Thy testimonies are my heritage for
   ever;
   yea, they are the joy of my heart.
112 I incline my heart to perform thy
   statutes
   for ever, to the end.

113 I hate double-minded men,
  but I love thy law.
114 Thou art my hiding place and my
  shield;
  I hope in thy word.
115 Depart from me, you evildoers,
  that I may keep the commandments of my God.
116 Uphold me according to thy promise, that I may live,
  and let me not be put to shame in
  my hope!
117 Hold me up, that I may be safe
  and have regard for thy statutes
  continually!
118 Thou dost spurn all who go astray
  from thy statutes;
  yea, their cunning is in vain.
119 All the wicked of the earth thou
  dost count as dross;
  therefore I love thy testimonies.
120 My flesh trembles for fear of thee,
  and I am afraid of thy judgments.

121 I have done what is just and right;
  do not leave me to my oppressors.
122 Be surety for thy servant for good;
  let not the godless oppress me.
123 My eyes fail with watching for thy
  salvation,
  and for the fulfilment of thy
  righteous promise.
124 Deal with thy servant according to
  thy steadfast love,
  and teach me thy statutes.
125 I am thy servant; give me understanding,
  that I may know thy testimonies!
126 It is time for the LORD to act,
  for thy law has been broken.
127 Therefore I love thy commandments
  above gold, above fine gold.
128 Therefore I direct my steps by all
  thy precepts;
  I hate every false way.

129 Thy testimonies are wonderful;
  therefore my soul keeps them.
130 The unfolding of thy words gives
  light;
  it imparts understanding to the
  simple.
131 With open mouth I pant,
  because I long for thy commandments.

132 Turn to me and be gracious to me,
  as is thy wont toward those who
  love thy name.
133 Keep steady my steps according to
  thy promise,
  and let no iniquity get dominion
  over me.
134 Redeem me from man's oppression,
  that I may keep thy precepts.
135 make thy face shine upon thy servant,
  and teach me thy statutes.
136 My eyes shed streams of tears,
  because men do not keep thy
  law.

137 Righteous art thou, O LORD,
  and right are thy judgments.
138 Thou hast appointed thy testimonies in righteousness
  and in all faithfulness.
139 My zeal consumes me,
  because my foes forget thy
  words.
140 Thy promise is well tried,
  and thy servant loves it.
141 I am small and despised,
  yet I do not forget thy precepts.
142 Thy righteousness is righteous for
  ever,
  and thy law is true.
143 Trouble and anguish have come
  upon me,
  but thy commandments are my
  delight.
144 Thy testimonies are righteous for
  ever;
  give me understanding that I
  may live.

145 With my whole heart I cry;
  answer me, O LORD!
  I will keep thy statutes.
146 I cry to thee; save me,
  that I may observe thy testimonies.
147 I rise before dawn and cry for help;
  I hope in thy words.
148 My eyes are awake before the
  watches of the night,
  that I may meditate upon thy
  promise.
149 Hear my voice in thy steadfast love;
  O LORD, in thy justice preserve
  my life.
150 They draw near who persecute me

with evil purpose;
they are far from thy law.
¹⁵¹But thou art near, O LORD,
and all thy commandments are
true.
¹⁵²Long have I known from thy tes-
timonies
that thou hast founded them for
ever.

¹⁵³Look on my affliction and deliver
me,
for I do not forget thy law.
¹⁵⁴Plead my cause and redeem me;
give me life according to thy
promise!
¹⁵⁵Salvation is far from the wicked,
for they do not seek thy statutes.
¹⁵⁶Great is thy mercy, O LORD;
give me life according to thy justice.
¹⁵⁷Many are my persecutors and my
adversaries,
but I do not swerve from thy testimonies.
¹⁵⁸I look at the faithless with disgust,
because they do not keep thy
commands.
¹⁵⁹Consider how I love thy precepts!
Preserve my life according to thy
steadfast love.
¹⁶⁰The sum of thy word is truth;
and every one of thy righteous
ordinances endures for ever.

¹⁶¹Princes persecute me without
cause,
but my heart stands in awe of thy
words.
¹⁶²I rejoice at thy word
like one who finds great spoil.
¹⁶³I hate and abhor falsehood,
but I love thy law.
¹⁶⁴Seven times a day I praise thee
for thy righteous ordinances.
¹⁶⁵Great peace have those who love
thy law;
nothing can make them stumble.
¹⁶⁶I hope for thy salvation, O LORD,
and I do thy commandments.
¹⁶⁷My soul keeps thy testimonies;
I love them exceedingly.
¹⁶⁸I keep thy precepts and tes-
timonies,
for all my ways are before thee.
¹⁶⁹Let my cry come before thee, O
LORD;

give me understanding according to thy word!
¹⁷⁰Let my supplication come before
thee;
deliver me according to thy
word.
¹⁷¹My lips will pour forth praise
that thou dost teach me thy statutes.
¹⁷²My tongue will sing of thy word,
for all thy commandments are
right.
¹⁷³Let thy hand be ready to help me,
for I have chosen thy precepts.
¹⁷⁴I long for thy salvation, O LORD,
and thy law is my delight.
¹⁷⁵Let me live, that I may praise thee,
and let thy ordinances help me.
¹⁷⁶I have gone astray like a lost sheep;
seek thy servant,
for I do not forget thy commandments.

A Song of Ascents.

120 In my distress I cry to the
LORD,
that he may answer me:
²"Deliver me, O LORD,
from lying lips,
from a deceitful tongue."

³What shall be given to you?
And what more shall be done to
you,
you deceitful tongue?
⁴A warrior's sharp arrows,
with glowing coals of the broom
tree!

⁵Woe is me, that I sojourn in Me-
shech,
that I dwell among the tents of
Kedar!
⁶Too long have I had my dwelling
among those who hate peace.
⁷I am for peace;
but when I speak,
they are for war!

A Song of Ascents.

121 I lift up my eyes to the hills.
From whence does my help
come?

2 My help comes from the LORD,
who made heaven and earth.

3 He will not let your foot be moved,
he who keeps you will not
slumber.
4 Behold, he who keeps Israel
will neither slumber nor sleep.

5 The LORD is your keeper;
the LORD is your shade
on your right hand.
6 The sun shall not smite you by day,
nor the moon by night.

7 The LORD will keep you from all
evil;
he will keep your life.
8 The LORD will keep
your going out and your coming
in
from this time forth and for evermore.

A Song of Ascents. Of David.

122 I was glad when they said to
me,
"Let us go to the house of the
LORD!"
2 Our feet have been standing
within your gates, O Jerusalem!

3 Jerusalem, built as a city
which is bound firmly together,
4 to which the tribes go up,
the tribes of the LORD,
as was decreed for Israel,
to give thanks to the name of the
LORD.
5 There thrones for judgment were
set,
the thrones of the house of David.

6 Pray for the peace of Jerusalem!
"May they prosper who love you!
7 Peace be within your walls,
and security within your towers!"

8 For my brethren and companions'
sake
I will say, "Peace be within you!"
9 For the sake of the house of the
LORD our God,
I will seek your good.

A Song of Ascents.

123 To thee I lift up my eyes,
O thou who are enthroned
in the heavens!
2 Behold, as the eyes of servants
look to the hand of their master,
as the eyes of a maid
to the hand of her mistress,
so our eyes look to the LORD our
God,
till he have mercy upon us.

3 Have mercy upon us, O LORD, have
mercy upon us,
for we have had more than
enough of contempt.
4 Too long our soul has been sated
with the scorn of those who are at
ease,
the contempt of the proud.

A song of Ascents. Of David.

124 If it had not been the LORD
who was on our side,
let Israel now say—
2 if it had not been the LORD who was
on our side,
when men rose up against us,
3 then they would have swallowed us
up alive,
when their anger was kindled
against us;
4 then the flood would have swept us
away,
the torrent would have gone over
us;
5 then over us would have gone
the raging waters.
6 Blessed be the LORD,
who has not given us
as prey to their teeth!
7 We have escaped as a bird
from the snare of the fowlers;
the snare is broken,
and we have escaped!

8 Our help is in the name of the LORD,
who made heaven and earth.

A Song of Ascents.

125 Those who trust in the LORD
are like Mount Zion,

which cannot be moved, but
    abides for ever.
2 As the mountains are round about
    Jerusalem,
    so the LORD is round about his
        people,
    from this time forth and for ever-
        more.
3 For the scepter of wickedness shall
    not rest
    upon the land allotted to the
        righteous,
    lest the righteous put forth
    their hands to do wrong.

4 Do good, O LORD, to those who are
    good,
    and to those who are upright in
        their hearts!
5 But those who turn aside upon their
    crooked ways
    the LORD will lead away with
        evildoers!
    Peace be in Israel!

A Song of Ascents.

126 When the LORD restored the
    fortunes of Zion,
    we were like those who dream.
2 Then our mouth was filled with
    laughter,
    and our tongue with shouts of joy;
    then they said among the nations,
    "The LORD has done great things
        for them."
3 The LORD has done great things for
    us;
    we are glad.

4 Restore our fortunes, O LORD,
    like the watercourses in the
        Negeb!
5 May those who sow in tears
    reap with shouts of joy!
6 He that goes forth weeping,
    bearing the seed for sowing,
    shall come home with shouts of joy,
    bringing his sheaves with him.

A Song of Ascents. Of Solomon.

127 Unless the LORD builds the
    house,
    those who build it labor in vain.

Unless the LORD watches over the
    city,
    the watchman stays awake in
        vain.
2 It is in vain that you rise up early
    and go late to rest,
    eating the bread of anxious toil;
    for he gives to his beloved sleep.

3 Lo, sons are a heritage from the
    LORD,
    the fruit of the womb a reward.
4 Like arrows in the hand of a warrior
    are the sons of one's youth.
5 Happy is the man who has
    his quiver full of them!
    He shall not be put to shame
    when he speaks with his enemies
    in the gate.

A Song of Ascents.

128 Blessed is every one who
    fears the LORD,
    who walks in his ways!
2 You shall eat the fruit of the labor of
    your hands;
    you shall be happy, and it shall be
    well with you.
3 Your wife will be like a fruitful vine
    within your house;
    your children will be like olive
    shoots around your table.
4 Lo, thus shall the man be blessed
    who fears the LORD.

5 The LORD bless you from Zion!
    May you see the prosperity of
        Jerusalem
    all the days of your life!
6 May you see your children's chil-
        dren!
    Peace be upon Israel!

A Song of Ascents.

129 "Sorely have they afflicted
    me from my youth,"
    let Israel now say—
2 "Sorely have they afflicted me from
    my youth,
    yet they have not prevailed
        against me.
3 The plowers plowed upon my back;
    they made long their furrows."

⁴The LORD is righteous;
he has cut the cords of the wicked.
⁵May all who hate Zion
be put to shame and turned
backward!
⁶Let them be like the grass on the
housetops,
which withers before it grows up.
⁷with which the reaper does not fill
his hand
or the binder of sheaves his
bosom,
⁸while those who pass by do not say,
"The blessing of the LORD be
upon you!
We bless you in the name of the
LORD!"

A Song of Ascents.

130 Out of the depths I cry to
thee, O LORD!
² Lord, hear my voice!
Let thy ears be attentive
to the voice of my supplications!

³If thou, O LORD, shouldst mark iniquities,
Lord, who could stand?
⁴But there is forgiveness with thee,
that thou mayest be feared.

⁵I wait for the LORD, my soul waits,
and in his word I hope;
⁶my soul waits for the LORD
more than watchmen for the
morning,
more than watchmen for the
morning.
⁷O Israel, hope in the LORD!
For with the LORD there is steadfast love,
and with him is plenteous redemption.
⁸And he will redeem Israel
from all his iniquities.

A Song of Ascents. Of David.

131 O LORD, my heart is not
lifted up,
my eyes are not raised too high;
I do not occupy myself with things
too great and too marvelous for
me.

²But I have calmed and quieted my
soul,
like a child quieted at its mother's
breast;
like a child that is quieted is my
soul.
³O Israel, hope in the LORD
from this time forth and for evermore.

A Song of Ascents.

132 Remember, O LORD, in
David's favor,
all the hardships he endured;
²how he swore to the LORD
and vowed to the Mighty One of
Jacob,
³"I will not enter my house
or get into my bed;
⁴I will not give sleep to my eyes
or slumber to my eyelids,
⁵until I find a place for the LORD,
a dwelling place for the Mighty
One of Jacob."

⁶Lo, we heard of it in Eph'rathah,
we found it in the fields of Ja'ar.
⁷"Let us go to his dwelling place;
let us worship at his footstool!"
⁸Arise, O LORD, and go to thy resting
place,
thou and the ark of thy might.
⁹Let thy priests be clothed with
righteousness,
and let thy saints shout for joy.
¹⁰For thy servant David's sake
do not turn away the face of thy
anointed one.

¹¹The LORD swore to David a sure
oath
from which he will not turn back:
"One of the sons of your body
I will set on your throne.
¹²If your sons keep my covenant
and my testimonies which I shall
teach them,
their sons also for ever
shall sit upon your throne."
¹³For the LORD has chosen Zion;
he has desired it for his habitation:
¹⁴"This is my resting place for ever;
here I will dwell, for I have desired it.

¹⁵I will abundantly bless her pro-
visions;
I will satisfy her poor with bread.
¹⁶Her priests I will clothe with salvation,
and her saints will shout for joy.
¹⁷There I will make a horn to sprout
for David;
I have prepared a lamp for my
anointed.
¹⁸His enemies I will clothe with
shame,
but upon himself his crown will
shed its luster."

A Song of Ascents.

133 Behold, how good and pleasant it is
when brothers dwell in unity!
²It is like the precious oil upon the
head,
running down upon the beard,
upon the beard of Aaron,
running down on the collar of his
robes!
³It is like the dew of Hermon,
which falls on the mountains of
Zion!
For there the LORD has commanded
the blessing,
life for evermore.

A Song of Ascents.

134 Come, bless the LORD,
all you servants of the LORD,
who stand by night in the house
of the LORD!
²Lift up your hands to the holy place,
and bless the LORD!

³May the LORD bless you from Zion,
he who made heaven and earth!

135 Praise the LORD.
Praise the name of the LORD,
give praise, O servants of the
LORD,
²you that stand in the house of the
LORD,
in the courts of the house of our
God!

³Praise the LORD, for the LORD is
good;
sing to his name, for he is gracious!
⁴For the LORD has chosen Jacob for
himself,
Israel as his own possession.

⁵For I know that the LORD is great,
and that our Lord is above all
gods.
⁶Whatever the LORD pleases he does,
in heaven and on earth,
in the seas and all deeps.
⁷He it is who makes the clouds rise at
the end of the earth,
who makes lightnings for the rain
and brings forth the wind from
his storehouses.

⁸He it was who smote the first-born
of Egypt,
both of man and of beast;
⁹who in thy midst, O Egypt,
sent signs and wonders
against Pharaoh and all his servants;
¹⁰who smote many nations
and slew mighty kings,
¹¹Sihon, king of the Amorites,
and Og, king of Bashan,
and all the kingdoms of Canaan,
¹²and gave their land as a heritage,
a heritage to his people Israel.

¹³Thy name, O LORD, endures for
ever,
thy renown, O LORD, throughout
all ages.
¹⁴For the LORD will vindicate his
people,
and have compassion on his servants.

¹⁵The idols of the nations are silver
and gold,
the work of men's hands.
¹⁶They have mouths, but they speak
not,
they have eyes, but they see not,
¹⁷they have ears, but they hear not,
nor is there any breath in their
mouths.
¹⁸Like them be those who make
them!—
yea, every one who trusts in
them!

19 O house of Israel, bless the LORD!
O house of Aaron, bless the LORD!
20 O house of Levi, bless the LORD!
You that fear the LORD, bless the LORD!

21 Blessed be the LORD from Zion,
he who dwells in Jerusalem!
Praise the LORD!

136 O give thanks to the LORD,
for he is good,
for his steadfast love endures for ever.
2 O give thanks to the God of gods,
for his steadfast love endures for ever.
3 O give thanks to the Lord of lords,
for his steadfast love endures for ever;

4 to him who alone does great wonders,
for his steadfast love endures for ever;
5 to him who by understanding made the heavens,
for his steadfast love endures for ever;
6 to him who spread out the earth upon the waters,
for his steadfast love endures for ever;
7 to him who made the great lights,
for his steadfast love endures for ever;
8 the sun to rule over the day,
for his steadfast love endures for ever;
9 the moon and stars to rule over the night,
for his steadfast love endures for ever;

10 to him who smote the first-born of Egypt,
for his steadfast love endures for ever;
11 and brought Israel out from among them,
for his steadfast love endures for ever;
12 with a strong hand and an outstretched arm,
for his steadfast love endures for ever;
13 to him who divided the Red Sea in sunder,
for his steadfast love endures for ever;
14 and made Israel pass through the midst of it,
for his steadfast love endures for ever;
15 but overthrew Pharaoh and his host in the Red Sea,
for his steadfast love endures for ever;
16 to him who led his people through the wilderness,
for his steadfast love endures for ever;
17 to him who smote great kings,
for his steadfast love endures for ever;
18 and slew famous kings,
for his steadfast love endures for ever;
19 Sihon, king of the Amorites,
for his steadfast love endures for ever;
20 and Og, king of Bashan,
for his steadfast love endures for ever;
21 and gave their land as a heritage,
for his steadfast love endures for ever;
22 a heritage to Israel his servant,
for his steadfast love endures for ever.

23 It is he who remembered us in our low estate,
for his steadfast love endures for ever;
24 and rescued us from our foes,
for his steadfast love endures for ever;
25 he who gives food to all flesh,
for his steadfast love endures for ever.

26 O give thanks to the God of heaven,
for his steadfast love endures for ever.

137 By the waters of Babylon,
there we sat down and wept,
when we remembered Zion.

² On the willows there
we hung up our lyres.
³ For there our captors
required of us songs,
and our tormentors, mirth, saying,
"Sing us one of the songs of
Zion!"

⁴ How shall we sing the LORD's song
in a foreign land?
⁵ If I forget you, O Jerusalem,
let my right hand wither!
⁶ Let my tongue cleave to the roof of
my mouth,
if I do not remember you,
if I do not set Jerusalem
above my highest joy!

⁷ Remember, O LORD, against the
E'domites
the day of Jerusalem,
how they said, "Rase it, rase it!
Down to its foundations!"
⁸ O daughter of Babylon, you devastator!
Happy shall he be who requites
you
with what you have done to us!
⁹ Happy shall he be who takes your
little ones
and dashes them against the rock!

A Psalm of David.

138 I give thee thanks, O LORD,
with my whole heart;
before the gods I sing thy praise;
² I bow down toward thy holy temple
and give thanks to thy name for
thy steadfast love and thy faithfulness;
for thou hast exalted above everything
thy name and thy word.
³ On the day I called thou didst answer me,
my strength of soul thou didst increase.

⁴ All the kings of the earth shall praise
thee, O LORD,
for they have heard the words of
thy mouth,
⁵ and they shall sing of the ways of
the LORD,
for great is the glory of the LORD.

⁶ For though the LORD is high, he regards the lowly;
but the haughty he knows from
afar.

⁷ Though I walk in the midst of trouble,
thou dost preserve my life;
thou dost stretch out thy hand
against the wrath of my
enemies,
and thy right hand delivers me.
⁸ The LORD will fulfil his purpose for
me;
thy steadfast love, O LORD, endures for ever.
Do not forsake the work of thy
hands.

To the choirmaster. A Psalm of David.

139 O LORD, thou hast searched
me and known me!
² Thou knowest when I sit down and
when I rise up;
thou discernest my thoughts from
afar.
³ Thou searchest out my path and my
lying down,
and art acquainted with all my
ways.
⁴ Even before a word is on my tongue,
lo, O LORD, thou knowest it altogether.
⁵ Thou dost beset me behind and before,
and layest thy hand upon me.
⁶ Such knowledge is too wonderful
for me;
it is high, I cannot attain it.

⁷ Whither shall I go from thy Spirit!
Or whither shall I flee from thy
presence?
⁸ If I ascend to heaven, thou art there!
If I make my bed in Sheol, thou art
there!
⁹ If I take the wings of the morning
and dwell in the uttermost parts of
the sea,
¹⁰ even there thy hand shall lead me,
and thy right hand shall hold me.
¹¹ If I say, "Let only darkness cover me,
and the light about me be night,"
¹² even the darkness is not dark to
thee,

the night is bright as the day;
for darkness is as light with thee.

¹³For thou didst form my inward
parts,
thou didst knit me together in my
mother's womb.
¹⁴I praise thee, for thou art fearful and
wonderful.
Wonderful are thy works!
Thou knowest me right well;
¹⁵ my fame was not hidden from
thee,
when I was being made in secret,
intricately wrought in the depths
of the earth.
¹⁶Thy eyes beheld my unformed sub-
stance;
in thy book were written, every
one of them,
the days that were formed for me,
when as yet there was none of
them.
¹⁷How precious to me are thy
thoughts, O God!
How vast is the sum of them!
¹⁸If I would count them, they are more
than the sand.
When I awake, I am still with
thee.

¹⁹O that thou wouldst slay the
wicked, O God,
and that men of blood would depart from me,
²⁰men who maliciously defy thee,
who lift themselves up against
thee for evil!
²¹Do I not hate them that hate thee, O
LORD?
And do I not loathe them that rise
up against thee?
²²I hate them with perfect hatred;
I count them my enemies.
²³Search me, O God, and know my
heart!
Try me and know my thoughts!
²⁴And see if there be any wicked way
in me,
and lead me in the way everlasting!

To the choirmaster. A Psalm of David.

140 Deliver me, O LORD, from
evil men;

preserve me from violent men,
²who plan evil things in their heart,
and stir up wars continually.
³They make their tongue sharp as a
serpent's,
and under their lips is the poison
of vipers. *Selah*
⁴Guard me, O LORD, from the hands
of the wicked;
preserve me from violent men,
who have planned to trip up my
feet.
⁵Arrogant men have hidden a trap for
me,
and with cords they have spread a
net,
by the wayside they have set
snares for me. *Selah*

⁶I say to the LORD, Thou art my God;
give ear to the voice of my supplications, O LORD!
⁷O LORD, my Lord, my strong deli-
verer,
thou hast covered my head in the
day of battle.
⁸Grant not, O LORD, the desires of
the wicked;
do not further his evil plot! *Selah*

⁹Those who surround me lift up their
head,
let the mischief of their lips overwhelm them!
¹⁰Let burning coals fall upon them!
Let them be cast into pits, no
more to rise!
¹¹Let not the slanderer be established
in the land;
let evil hunt down the violent man
speedily!

¹²I know that the LORD maintains the
cause of the afflicted,
and executes justice for the needy.
¹³Surely the righteous shall give
thanks to thy name;
the upright shall dwell in thy
presence.

A Psalm of David.

141 I call upon thee, O LORD;
make haste to me!
Give ear to my voice, when I call
to thee!

2 Let my prayer be counted as incense
before thee,
and the lifting up of my hands as
an evening sacrifice!

3 Set a guard over my mouth, O
LORD,
keep watch over the door of my
lips!
4 Incline not my heart to any evil,
to busy myself with wicked deeds
in company with men who work iniquity;
and let me not eat of their dain-
ties!

5 Let a good man strike or rebuke me
in kindness,
but let the oil of the wicked never
anoint my head;
for my prayer is continually
against their wicked deeds.
6 When they are given over to those
who shall condemn them,
then they shall learn that the word
of the LORD is true.
7 As a rock which one cleaves and
shatters on the land,
so shall their bones be strewn at
the mouth of Sheol.

8 But my eyes are toward thee, O
LORD God;
in thee I seek refuge; leave me not
defenseless!
9 Keep me from the trap which they
have laid for me,
and from the snares of evildoers!
10 Let the wicked together fall into
their own nets,
while I escape.

A Maskil of David, when he was in
the cave. A Prayer.

142 I cry with my voice to the
LORD,
with my voice I make supplication
to the LORD,
2 I pour out my complaint before him,
I tell my trouble before him.
3 When my spirit is faint,
thou knowest my way!

In the path where I walk
they have hidden a trap for me.

4 I look to the right and watch,
but there is none who takes notice
of me;
no refuge remains to me,
no man cares for me.

5 I cry to thee, O LORD;
I say, Thou art my refuge,
my portion in the land of the living.
6 Give heed to my cry;
for I am brought very low!

Deliver me from my persecutors;
for they are too strong for me!
7 Bring me out of prison,
that I may give thanks to thy
name!
The righteous will surround me;
for thou wilt deal bountifully with
me.

A Psalm of David.

143 Hear my prayer, O LORD;
give ear to my supplications!
In thy faithfulness answer me, in
thy righteousness!
2 Enter not into judgment with thy
servant;
for no man living is righteous before thee.

3 For the enemy has pursued me;
he has crushed my life to the
ground;
he has made me sit in darkness
like those long dead.
4 Therefore my spirit faints within
me;
my heart within me is appalled.

5 I remember the days of old,
I meditate on all that thou hast
done;
I muse on what thy hands have
wrought.
6 I stretch out my hands to thee;
my soul thirsts for thee like a
parched land.   *Selah*

7 Make haste to answer me, O LORD!
My spirit fails!
Hide not thy face from me,
lest I be like those who go down to
the Pit.

8 Let me hear in the morning of thy
 steadfast love,
 for in thee I put my trust.
Teach me the way I should go,
 for to thee I lift up my soul.

9 Deliver me, O LORD, from my
 enemies!
 I have fled to thee for refuge!
10 Teach me to do thy will,
 for thou art my God!
 Let thy good spirit lead me
 on a level path!

11 For thy name's sake, O LORD, preserve my life!
 In thy righteousness bring me out
 of trouble!
12 And in thy steadfast love cut off my
 enemies,
 and destroy all my adversaries,
 for I am thy servant.

A Psalm of David.

144 Blessed be the LORD, my
 rock,
who trains my hands for war,
 and my fingers for battle;
2 my rock and my fortress,
 my stronghold and my deliverer,
 my shield and he in whom I take
 refuge,
 who subdues the peoples under
 him.

3 O LORD, what is man that thou dost
 regard him,
 or the son of man that thou dost
 think of him?
4 Man is like a breath,
 his days are like a passing
 shadow.

5 Bow thy heavens, O LORD, and
 come down!
 Touch the mountains that they
 smoke!
6 Flash forth the lightning and scatter
 them,
 send out thy arrows and rout
 them!
7 Stretch forth thy hand from on high,
 rescue me and deliver me from the
 many waters,
 from the hand of aliens,

8 whose mouths speak lies,
 and whose right hand is a right
 hand of falsehood.

9 I will sing a new song to thee, O
 God;
 upon a ten-stringed harp I will
 play to thee,
10 who givest victory to kings,
 who rescuest David thy servant.
11 Rescue me from the cruel sword,
 and deliver me from the hand of
 aliens,
 whose mouths speak lies,
 and whose right hand is a right
 hand of falsehood.

12 May our sons in their youth
 be like plants full grown,
 our daughters like corner pillars
 cut for the structure of a palace;
13 may our garners be full,
 providing all manner of store;
 may our sheep bring forth thousands
 and ten thousands in our fields;
14 may our cattle be heavy with young,
 suffering no mischance or failure
 in bearing;
 may there be no cry of distress in
 our streets!
15 Happy the people to whom such
 blessings fall!
 Happy the people whose God is
 the LORD!

A Song of Praise. Of David.

145 I will extol thee, my God and
 King,
 and bless thy name for ever and
 ever.
2 Every day I will bless thee,
 and praise thy name for ever and
 ever.
3 Great is the LORD, and greatly to be
 praised,
 and his greatness is unsearchable.

4 One generation shall laud thy works
 to another,
 and shall declare thy mighty acts.
5 On the glorious splendor of thy
 majesty,
 and on thy wondrous works, I will
 meditate.

⁶Men shall proclaim the might of thy
  terrible acts,
and I will declare thy greatness.
⁷They shall pour forth the fame of thy
  abundant goodness,
and shall sing aloud of thy righteousness.
⁸The LORD is gracious and merciful,
  slow to anger and abounding in
  steadfast love.
⁹The LORD is good to all,
  and his compassion is over all that
  he has made.

¹⁰All thy works shall give thanks to
  thee, O LORD,
and all thy saints shall bless thee!
¹¹They shall speak of the glory of thy
  kingdom,
and tell of thy power,
¹²to make known to the sons of men
  thy mighty deeds,
and the glorious splendor of thy
  kingdom.
¹³Thy kingdom is an everlasting
  kingdom,
and thy dominion endures
  throughout all generations.

The LORD is faithful in all his words,
and gracious in all his deeds.
¹⁴The LORD upholds all who are falling,
and raises up all who are bowed
  down.
¹⁵The eyes of all look to thee,
and thou givest them their food in
  due season.
¹⁶Thou openest thy hand,
thou satisfiest the desire of every
  living thing.
¹⁷The LORD is just in all his ways,
and kind in all his doings.
¹⁸The LORD is near to all who call
  upon him,
to all who call upon him in truth.
¹⁹He fulfils the desire of all who fear
  him,
he also hears their cry, and saves
  them.
²⁰The LORD preserves all who love
  him;
but all the wicked he will destroy.
²¹My mouth will speak the praise of
  the LORD,
and let all flesh bless his holy
  name for ever and ever.

146 Praise the LORD!
    Praise the LORD, O my soul!
²I will praise the LORD as long as I
  live;
I will sing praises to my God
  while I have being.

³Put not your trust in princes,
  in a son of man, in whom there is
  no help.
⁴When his breath departs he returns
  to his earth;
on that very day his plans perish.

⁵Happy is he whose help is the God
  of Jacob,
whose hope is in the LORD his
  God,
⁶who made heaven and earth,
  the sea, and all that is in them;
who keeps faith for ever;
⁷ who executes justice for the oppressed;
who gives food to the hungry.

The LORD sets the prisoners free;
⁸ the LORD opens the eyes of the
  blind.
The LORD lifts up those who are
  bowed down;
the LORD loves the righteous.
⁹The LORD watches over the sojourn-
  ers,
he upholds the widow and the
  fatherless;
but the way of the wicked he
  brings to ruin.

¹⁰The LORD will reign for ever,
  thy God, O Zion, to all generations.
Praise the LORD!

147 Praise the LORD!
    For it is good to sing praises
  to our God;
for he is gracious, and a song of
  praise is seemly.
²The LORD builds up Jerusalem;
  he gathers the outcasts of Israel.
³He heals the brokenhearted,
  and binds up their wounds.
⁴He determines the number of the
  stars,
he gives to all of them their
  names.

5 Great is our LORD, and abundant in
power;
his understanding is beyond
measure.
6 The LORD lifts up the downtrodden,
he casts the wicked to the ground.

7 Sing to the LORD with thanksgiving;
make melody to our God upon the
lyre!
8 He covers the heavens with clouds,
he prepares rain for the earth,
he makes grass grow upon the
hills.
9 He gives to the beasts their food,
and to the young ravens which
cry.
10 His delight is not in the strength of
the horse,
nor his pleasure in the legs of a
man;
11 but the LORD takes pleasure in those
who fear him,
in those who hope in his steadfast
love.

12 Praise the LORD, O Jerusalem!
Praise your God, O Zion!
13 For he strengthens the bars of your
gates;
he blesses your sons within you.
14 He makes peace in your borders;
he fills you with the finest of the
wheat.
15 He sends forth his command to the
earth;
his word runs swiftly.
16 He gives snow like wool;
he scatters hoarfrost like ashes.
17 He casts forth his ice like morsels;
who can stand before his cold?
18 He sends forth his word, and melts
them;
he makes his wind blow, and the
waters flow.
19 He declares his word to Jacob,
his statutes and ordinances to Israel.
20 He has not dealt thus with any other
nation;
they do not know his ordinances.
Praise the LORD!

148 Praise the LORD!
Praise the LORD from the
heavens,

praise him in the heights!
2 Praise him, all his angels,
praise him, all his host!
3 Praise him, sun and moon,
praise him, all you shining stars!
4 Praise him, you highest heavens,
and you waters above the heavens!

5 Let them praise the name of the
LORD!
For he commanded and they were
created.
6 And he established them for ever
and ever;
he fixed their bounds which cannot be passed.

7 Praise the LORD from the earth,
you sea monsters and all deeps,
8 fire and hail, snow and frost,
stormy wind fulfilling his command!
9 Mountains and all hills,
fruit trees and all cedars!
10 Beasts and all cattle,
creeping things and flying birds!

11 Kings of the earth and all peoples,
princes and all rulers of the earth!
12 Young men and maidens together,
old men and children!

13 Let them praise the name of the
LORD,
for his name alone is exalted;
his glory is above earth and
heaven.
14 He has raised up a horn for his
people,
praise for all his saints,
for the people of Israel who are
near to him.
Praise the LORD!

149 Praise the LORD!
Sing to the LORD a new song,
his praise in the assembly of the
faithful!
2 Let Israel be glad in his Maker,
let the sons of Zion rejoice in their
King!
3 Let them praise his name with dancing,
making melody to him with timbrel and lyre!

⁴For the LORD takes pleasure in his people;
    he adorns the humble with victory.

⁵Let the faithful exult in glory;
    let them sing for joy on their couches.
⁶Let the high praises of God be in their throats
    and two-edged swords in their hands,
⁷to wreak vengeance on the nations
    and chastisement on the peoples,
⁸to bind their kings with chains
    and their nobles with fetters of iron,
⁹to execute on them the judgment written!
    This is glory for all his faithful ones.
    Praise the LORD!

150 Praise the LORD!
    Praise God in his sanctuary;
    praise him in his mighty firmament!

²Praise him for his mighty deeds;
    praise him according to his exceeding greatness!

³Praise him with trumpet sound;
    praise him with lute and harp!

⁴Praise him with timbrel and dance;
    praise him with strings and pipe!

⁵Praise him with sounding cymbals;
    praise him with loud clashing cymbals!

⁶Let everything that breathes praise the LORD!
    Praise the LORD!